THE MIRROR CRACK'D

THE MIRROR CRACK'D

When Good Enough Therapy Goes Wrong and Other Cautionary Tales for Humanistic Practitioners

*Edited
by
Anne Kearns*

KARNAC

First published in 2007 by
Karnac Books Ltd.
118 Finchley Road, London NW3 5HT

Copyright © 2007 byAnne Kearns/© 2007 All contributors

British Library Cataloguing in Publication Data

A C.I.P. for this book is available from the British Library

ISBN-13: 978-1-85575-423-2

Typeset by Vikatan Publishing Solutions, Chennai, India

Printed in Great Britain

www.karnacbooks.com

CONTENTS

Out flew the web and floated wide;
The mirror crack'd from side to side...
"I am half sick of shadows", said
The Lady of Shalott.
Tennyson

The range of what we think and do
Is limited by what we fail to notice
And because we fail to notice
That we fail to notice
There is little we can do
To change
Until we notice
How failing to notice
Shapes our thoughts and deeds.
R.D. Laing

ABOUT THE EDITOR

Anne Kearns is the author of *The Seven Deadly Sins: Issues in Clinical Practice and Supervision for Humanistic and Integrative Practitioners* (Karnac, 2005). She trained in psychoanalytic psychotherapy in the USA and in Transactional Analysis and Gestalt in the UK. She is a former Chair and Teaching and Supervising member of the Gestalt Psychotherapy & Training Institute. In 1999 she founded The Growing Edge, a consortium of psychotherapists and other professionals who are interested in the development of the profession of psychotherapy through post-qualification training and consultation. Anne has an MSc in Integrative Psychotherapy and was Course Director of the training in Integrative Group Therapy at the Metanoia Institute from 1994–96 and a Primary Tutor on the Integrative Psychotherapy training from 1994–1999. With Penny Daintry she is the author of "Shame in the Supervisory Relationship: Living with the Enemy" (*British Gestalt Journal*, Vol. 9, No.1, 2000). She is an academic advisor to the MSc in Gestalt Psychotherapy at the Metanoia Institute and teaches and supervises Gestalt and Integrative psychotherapists in the UK and abroad. Anne has a private practice in West London. She has been awarded the D Psych (Prof) from Middlesex University and the Metanoia Institute for her doctoral research in the areas of post-qualification training and procedural ethics. She is hoping to embark on a career in the law.

Teresa Bernier is a pseudonym. She is an integrative psychotherapist and writer with a particular interest in trauma. She has a private practice in London and may be contacted at the growing. edge@virgin.net

Tim Bond, PhD, Fellow of the British Association for Counselling and Psychotherapy, is currently the Reader in Counselling and Professional Ethics in the University of Bristol and in private practice providing therapy and supervision. He is an occasional trainer and consultant to the ethics committee of the Institute of Transactional Analysis (ITA) in the UK. He can be contacted at the Graduate School of Education, University of Bristol, 8–10 Berkeley Square, Bristol BS8 1HH; email: tim.bond@bris.ac.uk

Sue Jones is an integrative psychotherapist and Director of Training of Matrix College in East Anglia where she has been in private practice for over fifteen years. She has a particular interest in the development of training for counsellors and psychotherapists and the associated ethical framework. She is currently on the ethics committee of The United Kingdom Association of Therapeutic Counselling and is completing a doctorate on "A Psychotherapeutic Understanding of Organisational Function". She has recently been awarded the DPsych (Prof) from Middlesex University and the Metanoia Institute for her doctoral research on shadow and transparency in psychotherapy training institutes. Her email address is: sue@matrix-training.org

Patti Owens is a psychotherapist and supervisor in private practice in North London, and an Associate Lecturer in Arts at The Open

University. She is a former Board member of the UKAHPP and chaired the Ethics Committee in 2005. Trained as a Gestalt therapist, she now incorporates insights from attachment and relational theory and object relations therapy. Her earlier career was as a primary school teacher and university lecturer, and she is the editor of *Early Childhood Education and Care* (Stoke on Trent: Trentham, 1997). Her current research and writing focuses on developing a humanistic account of working with clients from an object relations perspective. Her email address is: contact@pattiowens.co.uk

Steven B. Smith, BA (Hons) Applied Social Sciences (Psychology & Sociology); BA (Hons) Christian Theology & World Religions; MSc Integrative Psychotherapy, is a UKCP Registered Integrative Psychotherapist and has been trained as an integrative and transpersonal supervisor.   He is interested in working with hateful and erotic impulses as they arise in the therapeutic dyad and as an integrative practitioner he is especially curious about the interface between the developmental ego and the transpersonal self. He is a primary tutor on the Counselling Psychology and Integrative Psychotherapy Department at the Metanoia Institute in Ealing. He has a private psychotherapy and supervisory practice in Fulham and can be contacted at: sbsmith01@aol.com

Bee Springwood first qualified as an Art Therapist in 1979, then trained in Body Psychotherapy in the 80's, and in Psychosynthesis with CCF. She is in private practice in Norfolk and Suffolk where she has also worked in statutory and community settings, including two NHS Trusts. Bee now co-leads Eastern Tree Training and Therapy, which is committed to creativity and integrity in training for counselling, art therapy, group work and mediation. Bee is registered as an Art Therapist with the Health Professions Council and is a UKCP registered psychotherapist. She joined the UKAHPP Ethics Committee in 1995 and was chair from 1999 to 2001. She is also, since 1995 been a member of Peering East, a member group of Independent Practitioners Network. She may be contacted at: springwood@onetel.com

PREFACE

I have been concerned for many years that the procedures governing ethical complaints against psychotherapists and counsellors in the UK do not adequately address the complexities of the therapeutic relationship, including the reality that psychotherapists and counsellors often work with people whose ability to relate has been significantly impaired and who present powerful challenges to the therapist and to the therapeutic relationship. I have also written of my concern that humanistic trainings are not preparing their trainees to work in the "real world". This, combined with humanistic psychotherapy's failure to address the power dynamics in the therapeutic relationship, does not equip the beginning therapist to offer the relational conditions that are necessary for effective psychotherapy nor does it support him to have a "healthy respect" for what is not in his nor the client's awareness or control (Kearns, 2005).

I've undertaken the project that resulted in this book for a number of reasons. The first is as a wake-up call to take seriously the climate in which we practise in which complaints and civil actions against psychotherapists and counsellors are on the increase and to sharpen assessment skills accordingly. The second is to help you to think about the "therapeutic frame" and what can happen to both the practitioner and the client when it is broken and finally to give voice to some colleagues who have been involved in the area of complaints in the hope that you and the organisations under whose codes of ethics you practise will take more of an interest in making those codes and frameworks more relevant to the intricacies of the therapeutic relationship. My message is brief: injuries that happen in relationship need to be addressed in relationship.

The book is divided into two parts. Part One includes chapters on the "Therapeutic Frame" and "Assessment and Risk Management", which were written with the aim of helping humanistic practitioners to think more clearly about boundary disturbances and about the kind of client with whom the therapist will need more than regular professional support. The chapter on "Love and Hate in the In-between" was written with Steven Smith in order to integrate concepts from psychoanalytic and object relations therapy with humanistic principles to offer practitioners an opportunity to deepen their thinking about erotic transference and countertransference. The last chapter in Part One is a lovely example of a therapist, Patti Owens, who supports her client through an impasse and potential rupture. I have included it here as evidence of what can be achieved when humanistic principles of autonomy and transparency are held alongside and are informed by a developmental perspective, diagnosis and clear contracting.

Part Two gives voice to people who have been involved in the area of ethical complaints. Theresa Bernier, an integrative psychotherapist, was willing to share her experience of being complained against, joining me in a call for governing bodies to consider mediation as a first step in any complaints procedure that does not involve gross professional misconduct such as sexual abuse or fraud. Bee Springwood, who also contributed some of her experience to the chapter on "The Therapeutic Frame" writes of her organisation, the ukAHPP's, journey towards and successful implementation of just such a system that offers support to both parties to a complaint. Sue Jones, who like me was doing research for a DPsych (Prof) through Middlesex University and the Metanoia Institute, was willing to share some of that here in a chapter that looks at the "shadow" in training organisations. She offers an example from her own organisation of how complaints and grievances are used as opportunities for dialogue and learning. Finally, Tim Bond writes about the risk and uncertainty that are inescapable existential challenges in counselling and psychotherapy and urges the profession to embrace an ethics of trust that will support the development of a more reciprocal professional relationship.

Many of the people who contributed to this book are not willing to be named, such is the culture of fear that surrounds the area of complaints in psychotherapy and counselling. I can, though, thank

Robert M. Young for his inspiration for the chapter on "The Therapeutic Frame" and for his sage advice on my research and Anna Waddell, who helped me with the magnificent cavern that is the British Library. I would also like to thank Pippa Weitz for commissioning this and *"The Seven Deadly Sins?"* Finally, I want to appreciate Jenifer Elton Wilson, Maja O'Brien, Mandy Kersey, Kate Maguire and Derek Portwood for their contributions to the doctoral programme sponsored by the Metanoia Institute and Middlesex University, and would like to particularly thank Kate and Derek for their support and patience.

CHAPTER ONE

The mirror crack'd

Anne Kearns

This book is the second to result from my work as a supervisor of humanistic and integrative psychotherapists. The first, *The Seven Deadly Sins?—Issues in Clinical Practice and Supervision for Humanistic and Integrative Practitioners* (Kearns, 2005) was based on a post-qualification course of the same name that was designed to address certain areas that I and colleagues had identified as under-discussed in the original training. Two of those areas–sexuality and erotic transference (Chapter Four) and money (Chapter Two)–were not included in my first book as they more naturally seemed to belong in this one as these are the areas where the misattunements that can become problematic often occur.

This book is the result of seven years of research towards a doctorate in psychotherapy. Before you begin to glaze over let me explain that when I say "research" I really mean that I talked to a lot of people. I first became interested in the vulnerability of psychotherapists and counsellors in 1997 when I was chair of my professional organisation and a representative to the HIPS section of the UKCP. Up until that point I hadn't really thought about the area of complaints. Suddenly I seemed to be submerged in it. In my role as chair of an organisation I struggled to keep the organisation in the UKCP as we had not followed our published procedures in a complaint that had been made against one of our founding members. As a representative to the HIPS section I became concerned that the HIPS section's own published procedures were un-thought-through and would lead to the escalation of disputes rather than containment, mediation and resolution.

Somehow I got known as a person who was interested in the organisational and interpersonal dynamics of complaints. People started "coming out of the closet" and talking to me about their experiences. I noticed that, despite the general agreement in the profession about the existence of transference phenomena (that the past is often re-enacted in the present), UKCP and BACP complaints procedures were not conceived in such a way as to contain those complainants who may, albeit unconsciously, be using their dissatisfaction with their therapist in order to take revenge on a figure from their past or to seek "justice". When this is the case I believe that entering into quasi-judicial procedures with a former therapist further injures both the client and the therapist, leading to more harm than was real or imagined in the therapy/counselling relationship. In the course of my doctoral research I came to see that practitioners were being traumatised and complainants were not finding the closure they were seeking. I soon realised that there were two types of complainant. The first seeks to challenge what they believe to be bad practice, often just wanting to be heard and for the "wrong" to be put right. Sometimes people in this category also want an apology from the therapist, or at least the therapist's admission that she has behaved unwisely or unethically. The second type of complainant wants more than to have a wrong put right or an apology. This type of complainant wants sanctions to be imposed, the therapist to be punished or "struck off". Increasingly she wants money. I became concerned that our complaints procedures themselves seemed to support what in some cases appears to be an almost insatiable thirst for justice or even revenge that is now more and more frequently being played out in civil actions against psychotherapists. Given the range of possibilities in the area of human disagreement this was alarming and interesting.

What was even more interesting was that those psychotherapists who had had–or feared they would have—a complaint made against them by the second type of complainant all told similar stories: the client had mentioned early in the therapy that there was someone or some organisation that they felt aggrieved by and were seeking some sort of compensation from; they also referred to hating or wanting to bring someone to justice, usually a parent or family member. Most had had some previous experience of psychotherapy and counselling and had found the practitioner less than adequate. In all but one instance the complaint was dropped but not before the therapist had spent months preparing for a hearing and an adjudication panel had been convened. I heard in these stories confirmation of my earliest concerns that the procedures governing complaints against humanistic and integrative psychotherapists and members of the BACP, having been designed in good faith in a genuine desire to protect the public, unwittingly caused harm to those practitioners who were complained against. It struck me as odd indeed that organisations that were training psychotherapists to operate from a philosophy that embraced transparency, respect and dialogue were not embodying those principles in their dealings with complaints.

My theoretical roots are in psychoanalytic theory but I have been most profoundly influenced by field theory (Lewin, 1952). When applied to the therapeutic relationship I believe that client and therapist are involved in a complex and interacting web of relationships, both past and present. There is no cause or effect; I and my environment and "action" and "re-action" are seen as part of a single system or whole. Each of us to a certain extent co-creates and reflects the other. What is not in our present awareness may be blocked by our past awareness; historic relationships impact on present relationships; a change in one part of the field impacts on the entire field.

The title for this book comes from a conversation I had with my hairdresser. I told him I was writing a book about complaints that result from a therapist's ordinary human error or temporary lack of judgement or even misattunement. He said, "But that's like taking the mirror back to the shop when you don't like what you see". The phrase "the mirror crack'd" comes from Tennyson's poem, "The Lady of Shalott". "The Lady of Shalott" is the story of a woman who lives in a tower on an island in the river that runs to Camelot, home of King Arthur and his Knights of the Round Table. She spends her days weaving a tapestry that depicts the landscape that she can see from her window. The problem is that there is a curse on the woman.

She doesn't know what caused the curse but she does know that as a result she can never look directly out the window. She needs a mirror to reflect the view and weave it into her tapestry. The Lady of Shallot enjoys her weaving but is tired of viewing the world around her as a mere reflection. One day, Sir Lancelot rides by and the woman goes to the window to see him. As she does so she realises that she is done for. The curse is upon her. So she leaves the tower, finds a boat and floats down the river towards Camelot singing and seeing all of the sights that had been forbidden to her before. Then she dies.

Agatha Christie also used the title "The Mirror Crack'd" for a thriller in which one of the guests at a summer tea party drops dead. It turns out that she was poisoned and that a visiting film star was the intended victim. In the discussions that led up to this book I became particularly interested in the kind of client who uses the therapeutic relationship to seek "revenge" on a figure from the past. Colleagues who have been complained against reported that they felt like their lives were being "poisoned" or "destroyed"; they also believed that they were not the "intended victim" but, rather, felt as though they were copping what belonged to an earlier significant other, usually mother.

The therapists who I talked to in more general terms about the whole area of complaints–the majority of whom were the participants on the Seven Deadly Sins training–shared an impression that their organisations' complaints procedures were "flawed" and in the same breath admitted that they had not exactly read their codes of ethics. Most of the therapists that I interviewed for my doctoral research and had had formal complaints made against them described the process as "traumatising" and "abusive" and the procedures as "naïve" at best and "dangerous" at worst. In most cases these practitioners were practising under the codes of ethics of a HIPS section (UKCP) organisation yet their practice had become increasingly influenced by more psychoanalytic concepts and procedures. The consensus was that organisations, in their zeal to protect the public from unscrupulous practitioners, have neglected to consider the need to protect the practitioner/organisation from vexatious complainants and from complaints that result from intractable negative transference.

Of the 70+ therapists who had *not* had complaints made against them only 6 were aware that the insurance they paid would not cover them unless they had legal action taken against them. (This is now changing and most insurers do provide some support in the preparation of a response to a complaint before it reaches the legal arena). They were also not aware that their professional organisations provided no formal or informal route to support a colleague who is complained against through the process of being complained against. Of those therapists who had been complained against all but one reported feeling like "a pariah", "in exile" "shunned" by their colleagues on ethics committees and/or investigation and adjudication panels. Of the therapists interviewed who had not had complaints taken out against them a worrying majority said that if it were to happen they would stop working as therapists.

Because complaints against psychotherapists and counsellors arise from a "private" relationship where one party seeks the other's help with matters that are both intimate and confidential it is easy to see how emotions can run high when a client feels let down by a therapist. It is also easy to see how a therapist can feel shamed and attacked when exposed to a panel of peers and accused of failures in good practice, particularly when those failures are the result—not of gross negligence, malice or intent to harm—but of ordinary human failing.

Psychotherapy is perhaps the only intimate professional relationship that exists almost entirely in private. When I go to the dentist his assistant is present. Any intimate or invasive examinations by a doctor are now very likely to be done in the presence of another. Penny Daintry and I have written earlier about shame phenomena in the supervisory relationship as arising from exposing aspects of this "private" relationship to a supervisor or colleagues, evoking the feeling of being spied on whilst having a very intimate experience (Kearns & Daintry, 2000; Kearns, 2005). I believe that the process of being complained against intensifies shame phenomena to a sometimes-crippling degree. It has been proposed (Guggenbuhl-Craig, 1971; Miller, 1981) that those of us who are drawn to the practice of psychotherapy have been narcissistically injured, and that one way of hiding this damage is to put ourselves in positions where we can help others. Benjamin (1996) believes that people with avoidant personality styles are attracted to the practice of psychotherapy because it provides an opportunity for intimacy from a safe distance.

I suspect that practitioners of the profession of psychotherapy have created a fertile breeding ground for shame through their historical reluctance to self-disclose. This was particularly true of the "blank screen" of the Freudian approach that influenced many theoretical orientations. Even Carl Rogers, whose early work was often described as "wooden", only described congruence as the most important and most difficult of the three Core Conditions relatively late in the development of the Person Centred Approach.

Therapists who have been through various complaints procedures describe the experience as "traumatising", "terrifying", "paralysing"–usually from the moment they received the letter from their professional organisation telling them that a former client had made a complaint. (For one therapist's experience see Chapter Five). What's going on? Linking the shame-inducing conditions mentioned above to the arena of complaints I have come to understand that the climate of fear that exists around complaints procedures is not just due to the procedures themselves being unsafe, which some certainly are, but to a more primitive reaction on the part of practitioners who feel, somehow, "caught out". Even if they haven't done anything wrong the process of public exposure of a kind of private relating that can never really be understood by an outsider, particularly when that outsider holds projections of father, judge and jury who are brought in to sort out "mother" who is left holding her client's projections of inadequacy is commonly experienced as deeply shaming.

Stokoe & Fisher (1997) see complaints from clients as an appeal to "Daddy" in the Oedipal triangle to put right what has gone wrong (see Chapter Four for a discussion of Oedipal issues as they impact the therapeutic relationship). They believe that, as clients come into therapy for help with containing what they cannot resolve on their own, the professional organisation *must* be a further source of containment and provide "therapeutic responses" for both client and therapist when things go wrong. In the experience of the people I interviewed that containment and "therapeutic response" was sorely missing.

In my conversations with people who have been involved in a complaint I have found that both the complainant and the person complained against in the course of the complaint being investigated experience a usually out of awareness rubbing up against their narcissistic wounds of each party. I believe that the rage of both parties is activated, as well as the practitioner's shame. On more than one occasion in my career I have attempted to support therapists who were clearly in the wrong to apologise to their clients in order to diffuse the situation. For a combination of reasons ranging from pride to fearing litigation they would not and both therapist and client suffered unnecessarily.

Kohut (1977) described the rage that seems to play a central role in the survival of the wounded self as "narcissistic rage". Firman and Gila (1997) write: "On a small scale, one can recognise rage in the automobile driver who becomes furious, irrational, and dangerous in response to the minor misdeeds of another driver ("road rage") or the impotent rage at not being able to find a mislaid personal possession..." (p. 174).

I have been concerned that clients experience unnecessary psychological damage, good enough practitioners abandon their careers and organisations fall into schism as the result of what appears to be a failure of professional organisations to recognise what Firman and Gila call "the Ahab complex", which I relate to the client who, due to the negative transference that can often result from therapeutic failures or misattunement, will unconsciously and usually self-righteously seek to "destroy" the therapist. In my discussion with psychotherapists and counsellors who have been involved in lengthy complaints all reported feeling as though the client wants to destroy them and at the same time to never let them go. Bollas (1987) writes of "loving hate" to describe how rage can be used to maintain an intimate connection, while at the same time appearing to want to destroy that connection. Whilst I do not want to give the impression that all complaints are fuelled by revenge and a desire for connection I do want to see procedures that govern complaints made against therapists to embrace a wider range of relational possibilities as opposed to assuming that if a client is taking the trouble to make a complaint the therapist must have done something wrong. Furthermore, I share Guthiel & Gabbard's (1998) concern that the codes–and I would add investigation or screening panels— that are designed to protect the client from "boundary violations" (see Chapter Two) are not adequately addressing the "context" in which an alleged violation occurs.

I have written earlier (Kearns, 2005) of my concern that humanistic trainings are turning out practitioners who may not be equipped to work in the "real world". I believe that in the current climate where we see a sharp increase in the number of complaints made against psychotherapists, good assessment and diagnostic skills and a commitment to learning more about our own "blind spots" are essential in order to protect the practitioner from complaints that are both emotionally and financially costly and draining. The participants in The Seven Deadly Sins? Training, the majority of whom had never been involved in a complaint, identified several areas that they wished had been addressed in more depth in their first training: assessment/diagnosis; contracting; erotic transference and money. Having said that my experience as a trainer of gestalt and integrative psychotherapists taught me the futility of attempting to teach into an abstraction. What I mean is that too often students are taught about concepts such as the working alliance, contracting, ethics and diversity *before* they are working with clients. I once had the experience of teaching a group of integrative trainees in their first year and again in their third. Many of these trainees showed no evidence of having learned what I taught them in year one. In fact they heartily denied that they *had* been taught about assessment, the initial interview and contracting. When we explored this together it emerged that, even in the third year of training, a majority were still not working with clients. Hebb's Axiom (1949) "use it or lose it" probably applies here.

Psychotherapy has been described as the intentional use of relationship (Metanoia Institute). In a speech at the Freud Museum's 1999 conference on the future of psychotherapy Lousada pessimistically anticipated that the "caring professions" may be veering towards a state of mind which itself is scared of forming relationships—the death knell, surely, of psychotherapy as we know it.

The practice of psychotherapy is just over 100 years old and humanistic psychotherapy is half that age. I believe that humanistic psychotherapy is in a stage of development that makes it particularly suggestible and vulnerable. I believe the way complaints are being handled reflects this developmental stage, which is akin to the latency or pre-adolescent phase in human development. Children in these years can be highly moralistic ("It's a sin to tell a lie") defensive and exclusive ("I'm not coming if she's coming!"). They tend to think the best of people.

I have been concerned for some time now that psychotherapy does not take itself seriously as a profession. Unlike psychologists we have no professional organisation to represent individual practitioners and the profession as a whole. The UKCP is a federal body with organisational, not individual, members. The BACP does have various categories of individual membership but, in my opinion, has procedures that over-zealously protect the public and, unconsciously support a collective *schadenfreude* that is evident in its tendency to rely on *prima facie* evidence without exploring associated transference phenomena, to progress complaints to adjudication without discussion with the therapist and in an alarming new policy of public shaming.

In the course of my research I identified a concern shared by practitioners who were registered in the HIPS section as well as BACP registered counsellors which was that the "bums on seats" approach to training gives the covert message that standards are not nearly as important as numbers (see Chapter Eight). Again and again people told me that they had been in training groups with people who seemed unsuited to the job for which they were training, either because they appeared to be too fragile or just not very good at relating to others. This market-driven approach to training seems to lie at the very heart of the difficulty we in the humanistic and integrative world seem to have in forming ourselves as a true profession, by which I mean a group of skilled specialists who respect each other as well as the people who come to us for help. As a supervisor I am increasingly concerned by the emphasis on short term therapy without an emphasis on the keen assessment skills that are essential to judging a client's suitability for short-term work. Furthermore I do not believe that a generation of psychotherapists who have done mainly short-term work as part of their training are being exposed to the sort of transference phenomena that more in-depth work supports. As a result when they meet a client who relates to them in overtly transferential ways they don't know how to deal with it.

I agree with Lee (2004), a gestalt therapist, who believes that people need to be seen and understood in the context of their own perspective and relational strivings. He also believes that the larger "field" (Lewin, 1952) of any relationship, clinical or personal, must be supported. He defines "health" as the ability to screen new experience as well as the ability to use new experience to test and to modify our ground, or what I call the historic relational field. Dysfunction is understood as the loss of ability to interact with others and the environment within a given field. I am concerned, and I want you to be concerned, about those clients for whom the experience that connection is not possible has become fixed. In my experience clients whose historic relational field includes betrayal, invasion, constant misattunement or punishment will seek to re-live these experiences with their therapist who needs to internalise and metabolise what is being presented in order for it to be re-worked in the therapeutic relationship. In order to do this the therapist must be able to tolerate a high degree of uncertainty and intense affect and needs a good deal of supervisory and other support from the present relational field, including other colleagues and his professional organisation.

A client whose historic relational field does not contain the possibility of support is also likely to have a present relational field outside the consulting room that is populated by unsupportive characters. The client may also use the environment in unsupportive ways and engage in active or passive self-harming behaviours. Such a client, no matter how much the therapist is supported to be able to work in a manner that is least likely to induce intolerable affect, may not be able to manage his or her own uncertainty and intense affect. Having "given" their projections to the therapist to metabolise, those projections may then be seen as inseparable from the therapist who may then be experienced as one and the same as a past oppressor and attacked from outside the consulting room, once the client chooses to leave, for inevitable and ordinary human frailty or what the client perceives as betrayal or rejection (See Chapter Three).

I have supported several practitioners through the process of being complained against by clients who could be described as having a ground that does not include room for the belief that connection or growth is possible and who could also be described as not experiencing their therapist's interventions and other non-verbal interactions as being supportive. I would like to see a professional relational field that embraces the principles of co-creation and support that is at the same time supported by the knowledge that some clients will not be able to be supported to stay in dialogue to work through their current and historic relational difficulties no matter how much the therapist is committed to and skilled in helping them to do so.

I take the view that relationships break down, even relationships between two well-intended people, both of whom need compassion and understanding. It seems to me paradoxical at best that a complaint of a "minor" failure in good practice can end up being referred to adjudication. I can easily admit to making minor failures in my practice, probably more than I realise. Experience has also shown me that "mistakes" often lead to healing and meeting.

As a supervisor and consultant to colleagues who have had complaints made against them I am all too aware that in cases that don't involve gross professional misconduct, complaints are usually made by clients who have left therapy in a state of dissatisfaction or of negative transference. Furthermore, although it is a notion unpopular in "humanistic" circles, I believe that these are often clients who have, out of awareness, entered therapy not to move on but to enact revenge on figures from their past; to play out their unfinished business in the therapeutic encounter rather than to complete it.

If I am correct in saying that these complaints arise mostly from a rupture in the working alliance and from negative transference then I believe that the only way to resolve them is in relationship, not in quasi-judicial proceedings. Of course the difficulty is that clients who are in negative transference or who are seeking "justice" are likely to be unwilling to enter into mediation.

I believe that the role of the ethics committees in these cases is to hold the client, to give assurance that the client's grievances are being taken seriously and to provide the client with enough support to "meet" the therapist, even if it is a meeting over time through correspondence, either by letter or email, rather than face-to-face. In Chapter Eight Bee Springwood writes about her organisation's experience of arriving at and implementing such a procedure.

Complaints need to be dealt with swiftly. The longer they are allowed to drag on and fester the more likely it becomes that the complainant–who already feels aggrieved–will become even more polarised and attacking. Conversely the person complained against is likely to become, understandably, more defensive. By the time complaints reach adjudication all possibility for dialogue is lost. Having mediation in some form as the first step in complaints that don't involve gross failures in good practice would, I believe, go some way towards addressing this polarisation. I do not believe that the imposition of sanctions would be necessary after the person complained against has gone through a process of mediation. Mediation and dialogue are transformative and help us to own our failings rather than to defend against them. Adjudication is by its very nature played out on an attack/defend continuum.

Totton (2001) has written that psychotherapy and counselling organisations have taken the "wrong road" in their approach to managing conflict between client and therapist, taking on a list of assumptions from other fields such as medicine and the legal system in addressing complaints (p. 99). As the profession moves towards statutory regulation of psychotherapists I am saddened to see that the UKCP's description of the Independent Complaints Organisation that will administer complaints against psychotherapists seems top-heavy and complex and favours words such as "judicial" and "evidence" over "mediation". Even the law is recognising the value of mediation as a means of conflict resolution—particularly in divorce and family disputes—because it is faster, less traumatic and more cost effective than adversarial litigation. According to the British Association of Lawyer Mediators, because of its advantages mediation is also becoming increasingly popular in the resolution of neighbourhood, labour and employment and personal injury cases. It is paradoxical at best that psychotherapists, who possess the skills necessary to support effective mediation, are not being supported to use them.

In Chapter Nine Tim Bond writes of a need for the profession of counselling and psychotherapy to embrace trust-based ethics. In my view we need to do a great deal of groundwork in order for that to happen. We need to pay more attention to training professionals who are well equipped *and* who have basic trust and respect for each other. We need to develop professional organisations that support the practitioner. If it is not possible within the current climate of accountability and consumer care for the organisations we *do* have to represent us at the moment—the UKCP and the BACP—to evolve to do this then we need new organisations. It may be that the roles of regulation and support need to be separated and that we need to be creative about what an organisation that only supports practitioners would look like. In the short-term we need to ensure that the organisations who do represent us have procedures in place that reflect an understanding of the subtler elements of human relating and of the field conditions that impact on relationships when they break down. I hope that I and the colleagues who have joined me in this book can stimulate you to think about how to make those things possible whilst, in the meantime, adjusting your practice to put yourselves and your clients at less risk in the current climate.

CHAPTER TWO

The therapeutic frame: "good fences make good neighbours" (Robert Frost)

Anne Kearns

As a supervisor of humanistic and integrative practitioners I have often struggled in helping them to move from what appears to be a more social relationship to a professional and therapeutic way of relating that includes a deeper understanding of the unspoken dynamics of the therapeutic relationship that can easily get played out in the transference/countertransference relationship. I have been concerned for some time that what I believe to be the "myths" of mutuality and horizontality and the emphasis of process-oriented therapies on congruence (Rogers, 1951) or on presence and open and clear communication (Hycner & Jacobs, 1995) has taken humanistic practitioners away from a clinical focus the very real difference between client and therapist.

In my experience true mutuality is not possible in any relationship where one party has ultimate responsibility for another. When that is so it is not possible to give the experience of each party "equal" weight. As much as the therapist must bring humanity and humility to the encounter we must be vigilant not to let the common ground that we share with our clients lead us to lose sight of the fact that we have responsibilities in the relationship that are different from the client's responsibilities. The therapist needs to attend to her experience in the room, moment by moment, but also needs to "bracket" all sorts of thoughts and feelings and impulses. The client has no obligation to do this. In fact we actively encourage our clients to bring us their deepest thoughts and feelings. We also insist on some level that they control their impulses when in the room with us. It would not, for example, be acceptable for a client to hit their therapist or to damage his property. We control the boundaries of time and payment.

Furthermore with the "professionalisation" of psychotherapy and counselling and the accompanying codes of ethics and practice our clients have power over us that we do not have over them. They can—and more and more frequently do—take out complaints that are not based on gross professional misconduct like sexual or financial impropriety but rather on perceived misattunement and ordinary, human frailty that can neither be proven by the client nor defended by the therapist. More alarmingly some of these complaints, even where the practitioner has been exonerated by the professional organisation, are now ending up in court.

Humanistic psychotherapy's failure to address the power dynamics in the therapeutic relationship goes hand in hand with its philosophical refusal to accept "dysfunction". Rowan (2001) describes the humanistic view of the client as being like a plant, which given the right conditions, will thrive. I don't entirely disagree. But I have had the experience of tending plants, giving them sunlight and water and food, only to watch them wither from a "disease" that has taken hold at the roots. Even though all energy is potentially creative, creativity can and does get subverted into a less-than-positive energy that turns against self and other. I believe that an effective psychotherapist needs to be skilled at offering relational conditions *and* needs also to have a healthy respect for what is not in his or the client's awareness or even control. This process gets played out in unconscious or non-verbal communication between therapist and client. What's needed is more sophisticated thinking about the *clinical* use of the core conditions and the *clinical* application of the components of the dialogic relationship, particularly regarding the use of self-disclosure.

Humanism, with its emphasis on here and now relationship and process, seems to lack a language to describe the therapeutic space or "frame" and its function in the aspect of psychotherapy that is a professional, contractual "service". It is not unusual for therapists in the

UK to work at home. Nor is it unusual for humanistic therapists to work with the client outside, either because the original contract includes this as an option or, as a supervisee has just told me, because "it was too hot in the office". I tried to help this supervisee see that, by taking a client outside into her garden, she forfeited her ability to offer the client a protected, confidential space that is as free as is possible from intrusion. I did not succeed. Later on today a colleague who comes to me for supervision expressed her despair about her inability to help her supervisee to see how he might be putting himself at risk when, after discovering that the consulting room that he rents was occupied by another therapist, he suggested to his attractive female client that they "do the therapy in the car". And they did.

I want to stress that the boundaries of the therapeutic frame are not just there for the client's benefit but are also indispensable components of the therapist's support and protection. Casemore (2001, pp. 113–4) has written that breaching boundaries is one of the most common causes cited in complaints to the BACP and that the majority of these complaints are against therapists who describe themselves as person centred. He goes on to say that he believes that boundaries have to be deliberately activated and monitored by the therapist (p. 114). My colleagues who supervise person centred trainees and newly-qualified person centred counsellors report that those less-experienced person centred practitioners seem to zealously believe that Rogers's core conditions of empathy, congruence and unconditional positive regard are all that is "necessary and sufficient" for change to take place. They may not be aware that Rogers' also included in his "basic hypothesis" the necessity for a "definitely structured, permissive relationship" (1942, p. 18). A supervisee who runs a counselling service with students from different courses on placement recently told me that her person centred students were being taught that the client should be able to dictate the boundaries of the counselling relationship to the extent that the client and *only* the client should decide at what time the session begins and how long it lasts. My colleague was dismayed, as was I, to discover that there is person centred literature to support this (Perraton Mountford, 2005).

What follows are my reflections on how to think about and maintain what psychoanalytic psychotherapists call the analytic frame. I am grateful for the contributions made by my colleague and research supervisor, Robert M Young, a psychoanalytic psychotherapist, in a lecture given at the Centre for Psychotherapeutic Studies, University of Sheffield and in subsequent discussions in helping me to focus my thinking here.

"Good fences make good neighbours"

Milner used the phrase "analytic frame" to make an analogy between providing boundaries for the therapeutic work and setting and a picture frame. (Milner, 1952, p. 183). Some years later Bleger wrote of the therapeutic encounter: "This situation comprises phenomena which constitute a *process* ... but it also includes a *frame*, that is to say, a "non-process", in the sense that it is made up of constants within whose bounds the process takes place". (Bleger, 1967, p. 511) I hope to help you to think beyond process to those non or not-entirely process elements that make up the therapeutic frame.

There are many aspects of the "frame" in psychotherapy. I like to think of it not just as the boundary around the work but as the structure and arrangements that support it, like a Zimmer frame, and contain it like a playpen or a fence. Sometimes when I walk in the country I find fences a burden; if I were a farmer I would see them as absolutely essential to my livelihood.

The frame is more than a room or a physical setting. It is also a set of conventions about how the therapist should conduct his practice. It is a state of mind—a mental space. It is all of these at once and something more, something ineffable. It has been described as the "holding environment" (Winnicott, 1967) and as a "container" (Bion, 1959). It needs to be a safe enough place for psychotherapeutic work to occur, a place where clients can feel able to speak about things that are too painful or taboo or shameful to speak about elsewhere. Perls, the founder of gestalt therapy, talked about the "safe emergency", referring to the experimental conditions in the therapeutic relationship that provide enough safety for something new to emerge. Contemporary gestalt theorists have come to see that this is a challenge for the practitioner who is working with clients whose self-process is fragile. Philippson, using the metaphor of "play", reminds us that building up a sense safety is slow with those clients, who do not play (schizoid), or do not play safely (borderline), or do not play as partners (narcissistic). This also takes time where trust is absent, or perception is heavily distorted by projection (Philippson, 2002).

The essence of the safety of the space is that the client can communicate thoughts and feelings—not necessarily verbally—to the therapist, which are held and processed by the therapist and given back in due course in a form that can be held and processed in awareness by the client, leading to integration and change.

Any attempt to list all the factors making up the "frame" in psychotherapy, would leave something out and would fail to capture its essence. Such is the nature of human relating. The things I will spell out are just examples, designed to get you thinking. The point is that the frame should make the therapeutic space which it bounds as a suitable place for the work. It should be quiet and as free as possible of the sort of interruptions that are in the therapist's control such as answering phone calls or the doorbell. It should not have the sort of pictures or other mementoes in view that reveal personal matters or relationships. It should be pleasant and comfortable. It should, as far as possible, remain the same.

The working alliance

In part, the therapeutic frame takes the form of a contract about what the client can and cannot expect and what the therapist will and will not do, will or will not allow. In this sense it includes the ground rules and mutual agreements that will form the basis of the working alliance. This is comprised of the customs and practices that have developed over the history of psychotherapy, such as the 50 minute hour as well as specific and contractual arrangements about payment, frequency and cancellation policies that are different for different therapists and schools of therapy. The working alliance also refers to the shared goals, bonds and tasks (Bordin, 1994) that the client and therapist develop over time. It is the part of the therapeutic relationship where the client and therapist on some level say, "Can we get down to business?" It also creates the sense that client and therapist are engaged in a shared enterprise and will support the client to hang in there even when they want to run away. This is also known as the observing ego. Clients who haven't got a well-developed observing ego can not form a working alliance. With people like this, sometimes described as "borderline", forming the working alliance is the goal of the therapy and not the structure that supports it (Masterson, 1988).

Bob and I, even though we come from different philosophical and theoretical positions, can agree on a number of "givens" about the therapist's behaviour and demeanour. She should answer the door promptly and begin and end the session on time. Self-disclosure should be used only when it contributes to the therapy and never gratuitously or self-indulgently. Session times should not be changed unless absolutely necessary and with as much notice as possible. Information about breaks or fee changes should be given well in advance. Timing is crucial to the maintenance of the frame, not just session timing but the timing of changes to the contract of the pace of the work. Two of the complaints that I have read involve allegations that the therapist announced fee increases or other changes to the "frame" just before a long break, allegedly causing the client undue anxiety. One also alleges that the therapist opened up a new and difficult area of exploration and then announced that he was taking an unscheduled holiday.

Confidentiality

Confidentiality is another component of the therapeutic frame. In the current climate it is a good idea to spell out to clients with whom the work will be discussed and how. This is particularly important for trainee therapists who may be expected to use case material for their written work and for examination purposes. It is also a good idea to let clients know that the law is specific about some exceptions to confidentiality and to let them know the requirements of your codes of ethics that govern your behaviour when speaking to other professionals about the therapy. There are some things about which neither the law nor ethical codes are specific. Some trainees are told that they must ask the client for their GP's phone number in order to be able to liase in the event that the therapist believes the client to be at risk.

Bond (2002) gives a hypothetical example of how lack of clarity concerning the limits to confidentiality could put the practitioner at serious risk. A 23 year old university student seeks counselling because she has become so distraught by the break-up of a relationship that she has begin having regular thoughts about wanting to die. She enters counselling determined not to act on those feelings but realising that she needs someone to talk things through with, someone with whom she can be honest and open. The counselling service advertises itself as being "confidential". The counsellor suggests to his client that she talk to her GP. The client rejects this suggestion, as she is concerned that the word "suicide" on her medical records might adversely affect her future career choice; in fact she has deliberately chosen to see a counsellor in a neutral setting in order to avoid her suicidal ideation going on her medical records. She also says that she is confident that she will not kill herself. The counsellor insists that if the client did not consult with her GP he will do so. The counsellor did consult the GP with the consequence that his client's future career *was* adversely affected.

In this example the counsellor's anxiety and over-zealous adherence to what he had been taught led him to take action that was not in the client's—or his—best interest.

Technology–friend or foe?

The therapeutic frame is not confined to the room where the therapy is done. It needs to be tacitly in the therapist's mind whenever he has contact with the client. It is there when a therapist opens the door or speaks to a client on the phone. It is conveyed by the therapist's demeanour, tone of voice, pauses, silences, grunts as well as in the wording of any note or letter or text or email. Technology is providing new challenges to the maintenance of the therapeutic frame. I have more than once been concerned about a supervisee's own boundaries being violated by clients who have been given email addresses and mobile phone numbers. In my experience clients whose ability to tolerate separation has been damaged in infancy, as well as those who find it hard to wait for what they want *now*, may abuse access to the therapist through emails and texts. These ways of communicating take an element of the personal out of "talking". Someone who may think twice about making a phone call to his therapist on a Sunday evening may not exercise the same reflective restraint when it comes to sending texts. Several texts, even. Many of my colleagues who work from home and would agree that having separate phone lines is essential to keeping work issues from intruding on private time and space, are also finding that they now give a different email address to their clients from the one they use to communicate with friends and family so they can have more control over intrusions. The same goes for mobile numbers. I know several therapists who use a "pay as you go" option for a mobile that they only use for client contact.

This may sound a bit excessive but I know of more than one therapist who put in another phone line after answering what they were sure was a personal call, received after midnight, in an intimate way only to discover that a client was on the other end. Other colleagues report sending personal emails or texts accidentally to clients whose name came just before or after the intended recipient in their "address book". Think about it.

Boundary disturbances

Acting out, or what more humanistic or existential therapists may describe as a "boundary disturbance" can be understood as challenging or breaking the therapeutic frame. There are many fairly routine examples of acting out: not coming to sessions, unnecessarily phoning the therapist, bringing inappropriate gifts, messing around with payment, refusing to speak, coming early or refusing to leave at the end of the session, shouting, screaming, preventing the therapist from speaking, dressing provocatively, acting seductively, lying, bringing inappropriate things to the session (e.g., a bottle of wine, tape recorder), taking an unplanned holiday just before or after the therapist's holiday.

The therapist's emotional and somatic experience or countertransference in the face of these boundary disturbances needs to be understood as one of the components of the therapeutic frame. One feature of a boundary disturbance is that the therapist is usually put under pressure to do something he would not otherwise do—to go after the client in some way, e.g., to write or phone, to reveal something, to move, to wait, to change a session, to confront, to relent about a decision or take a firm line, even to lose his temper. I have come to believe that within the therapeutic relationship *any* boundary disturbance conveys an implicit message. The job of the therapist is to metabolise the message in order to help the client to make that message explicit. Of course all instances of lateness are not necessarily fraught with meaning. In London where I live the traffic *is* challenging and unpredictable; the underground shuts down for all sorts of reasons. Still, even if a client has a perfectly good reason for being late, even including events out of her control, she may also, out of her aware-ness, relate to that explanation in a way that masks a more implicit, encoded message that she can find no other way of conveying.

A colleague had a client who used regularly to come very late to sessions. When asked why she thought she did this she offered all sorts of explanations–traffic, sick kids, a long wait at the dentist. The therapist mentioned in supervision that she felt like she spent more time waiting for the client than she did *with* the client. Her supervi-sor wondered aloud one day if the client might find the feeling of being kept waiting so hard to bear that the lateness was a way to assure that the therapist would always be there *waiting for her* and would come quickly to the door. When the therapist offered this to the client as a possibility the therapy moved through a long impasse to a fruitful exploration of the client's experience as a child who was often left to wait in the school yard to be collected long after the other children had been taken home.

Self-disclosure

The therapist's self-disclosure is a key element involved in the main-tenance of the therapeutic frame. Myers (2005) believes that self-dis-closure may be the most fundamental element of psychotherapy. Regardless of the therapist's theoretical orientation, he believes that it is a given that it is not "therapy" unless some form of communi-cation from the therapist is taking place. We can't be in relationship–any relationship–without revealing something of ourselves. The question we need to ask ourselves is how much do we reveal and when and why.

A recent study involving psychology students at Pennsylvania State University revealed that, when the working alliance was weak, disclosures on the part of the "therapist" led the "client" to evaluate the therapist's expertise in a negative manner. On the other hand, when the working alliance was judged to be strong the therapist was viewed more favourably when he *did* self-disclose (Myers, 2005).

It would seem that the therapist's ability to judge the strength of the working alliance is key to making self-disclosures that move the therapy along rather than become stuck in an impasse. Practitioners need to consider this when making even theoretically supported self-disclosures early on in the therapy. A supervisee, when listening to a new client tell a story of a pretty terrible life, disclosed that she felt touched by his bravery. He didn't return to the next session and could not be persuaded to come back. He did, though, write to the therapist and say that he had a hard enough time dealing with his own feelings and had been put off by having to hear about hers.

The choice about when and what to disclose to a client must be a *technical* choice and not done spontaneously or intuitively. But even a well-considered technical choice can misfire. A colleague who describes herself as a recovering alcoholic and who has not had a drink in over 20 years met a new client who described various difficulties in managing her relationship with alcohol and other recreational drugs. My colleague chose to disclose that she had been through a similar struggle in her 30s. The client seemed relieved to hear this and the therapy continued for several years with the therapist often sharing her experience of her struggles with alcohol.

The client improved and all seemed on track until real life intervened. The therapist came down with flu at the weekend and, as she felt too ill to ring her clients to cancel their sessions that week, asked a colleague to do it for her. The colleague phoned the client on the Monday to cancel her session for that evening, explaining that her therapist was ill and would see her at the regular time the following week. She seemed to take this in her stride but, when she saw her therapist again, she was in a rage. Weeks went by with the client becoming more and more convinced that the therapist had cancelled the session, not because she had flu, but because she had been drunk. The client eventually ended the therapy and, a year later, made a formal complaint to the therapist's membership organisation in which she alleged that my colleague used the therapy to work out her own struggles with alcohol, frequently cancelled sessions because she was the worse for wear and was, on more than one occasion, drunk in the session. The ethics committed suggested a meeting between the two, which the client refused, and the matter was not taken further as the therapist's colleagues knew of her commitment to sobriety and did not believe the client's allegations. As I understand it the client is now considering legal action against the therapist *and* the ethics committee.

Let me give you another example. A colleague of mine tells the story of an assessment session that had an unusual outcome. The client was a very successful architect. He was self-referred and told the therapist that he believed he needed to sort himself out because for years, each time he finishes a project, he goes into a decline and takes to his bed for about three months. When questioned by the therapist he said that it was more like two weeks he spent in bed; then he usually feels well enough to drag himself to the GP for some anti-depressants. The therapist asked the client if he was aware of being angry with anyone, in his life now or from the past. The client said that he was indeed furious with his business partner who had embezzled £40,000 from him and that he frequently fantasised about burning down this woman's house so that she can experience some of the anguish that the client and his wife have experienced. He asked the therapist if he thought this was "crazy". The therapist replied that if someone stole that much money from her she could imagine feeling as angry as the client did. Several days later the therapist received a phone call from the client's wife who said, "Did you tell my husband that it was ok for him to set fire his partner's house?"

Apparently the client has left the assessment session and attempted to set fire to his business partner's garage. Oops.

When I feel inclined to disclose something about myself, from telling the client how I am feeling impacted to using a personal anecdote to support the work, I find it useful to consider from where in me the impulse to self-disclose is emerging. As I see it there are four "places" in me from which the impulse to disclose something about myself arises. When it begins to seem to me like a good idea to share something about my own experience or about how I am being impacted in the moment I do a split-second check of the following possibilities:

Am I being invited to be with my client in a way that an important figure in her past has been or should have been? For example, with Flicka I frequently feel that too much is being asked of me. I don't share this with her as I imagine that that is how her mother used to feel and I used it as information to support a more holding intervention. Rather than succumb to the invitation to agree with Flicka's self-attacking belief that she is too difficult, I tell her that I notice how hard she works to get me to agree with mother and others that she is impossible but that I am not going to join the chorus.

Am I thinking about sharing this because I am in some sort of competition with my client? A colleague who is hoping to have a screenplay accepted–someday—confesses that she is likely to offer stories of her struggles with creativity, particularly to clients who she sees as more successful in that department than she may be.

Is this coming from my own need, to relieve boredom or to avoid conflicts? I have to watch myself from disclosing something about how I am feeling in order to fill silences that make *me* uncomfortable but are supportive of the work. Whilst I believe that sharing my own experience with certain clients can be healing I also need to watch that I am not offering unhelpful reassurance on the one hand or a tacit instruction to the client that I can't take her envy or aggression.

Am I responding in the here and now to a here and now invitation from the client? As much as I believe that clients have real questions and curiosity that deserve a straightforward response from me, I also believe that my clinical responsibility is to anticipate, through checking what I know (or don't) of the client's history and what is being evoked in me, what may be behind even a simple question. The heterosexual male client of a colleague who is a gay man said, apparently casually and after several years of therapy, "I heard that you're gay? Is that true?" The therapist, knowing that his sexuality was no secret in his professional network said that it was indeed true. This threw the therapy into a negative spiral from which it never recovered, the client in the transference believing that the therapist was trying to seduce him. This ended up in a complaint to the therapist's professional organisation that has still not been resolved.

Boundary violations

Guthiel and Gabbard (1998) define a boundary as the edge of appropriate behaviour. We might say that maintaining professional boundaries is a "given" to effective practice. But humanistic therapies have not developed a discourse as to *why* those boundaries are important. Practitioners, whatever, their theoretical orientation, need to maintain professional boundaries that will not be crossed, not to come across as rigid, but in order that *psychological* boundaries may effectively be crossed (Guthiel & Gabbard, 1998, p. 3) through empathy and its components projection and identification. In other words we can't practise empathy or its close relative, inclusion, without entering the client's world; and we must allow our clients to enter our thoughts and feelings in order to help us to hold and process for them that which they cannot yet know.

In the next chapter, "Assessment and Risk Management", we will look in more depth at a client called Gretl, who a supervisee has just introduced to me. She is 45 and is recently estranged from her husband of 20 years. They have three children–two daughters and a son. Gretl describes herself as "having woken up at 40". She tells the story of attending a personal development weekend with a friend and "realising" that she had been living her life since the age of 13 in denial of having been sexually abused by her older brother every time he came home from university and they were alone in the house. After university he moved to Australia following a year of travelling and she has had very little contact with him since.

Gretl's husband left the family home three years ago following Gretl's continuing allegations that he had "behaved inappropriately" with their youngest daughter. The daughter denies this but Gretl believes that she is in denial like she was. A year after her husband moved out a young woman was murdered in a nearby village. After hearing the details of the murder and the police's profile of the murderer Gretl went to the police and told them that she believed her husband could be the person they were looking for. They did not take their inquiries further and Gretl has not told anyone but a previous counsellor that she went to the police with her concerns. Gretl describes her former counsellor as having been inadequate in various ways, which include not being experienced enough to work with the complex issues she was presenting.

My supervisee feels warmly disposed towards Gretl and looks forward to working with her. I feel increasingly anxious and notice that my heart is beating faster than usual. I ask her how she feels towards her predecessor and she seems startled. I persist. She replies, "If I'm honest I feel a bit superior to her–like *I* will succeed where *she* has failed".

Gabbard (2000, pp. 211–212) has written that practitioners who engage in boundary violations with their clients often lose sight of the phenomenon of transference. They begin to emphasize the "real" relationship and feel that their uniqueness as a human being is *the* therapeutic factor in the treatment rather than their knowledge or technique.

In her study of the use of self in psychotherapy Cooper-White (2001) found that therapists found justification for overstepping the boundaries of professional relating by calling on the "real relationship". She warns that the recognition of our common grounding in the human condition can lead too easily to a facile explanation of the loosening of boundaries in the name of mutuality (p. 21) The term "real relationship" was introduced by Greenson (1978), a psychoanalyst, who used it to refer to those aspects of therapeutic relating that might be understood as separate from the transference. Alexander's (1948) concept of the "corrective emotional experience" has crept into humanistic discourse and is often misused to give theoretical support for the therapist's offering what Barr (1987) called the "developmentally needed relationship" by giving the client what the client says he didn't get when he was a child. When I was a trainee a popular catch-phrase introduced by one of the trainers was "It's never too late to have a happy childhood", as though psychotherapy could erase the past and create a new life in the present. Through concepts such as "re-parenting" (Schiff & Day, 1970) and experiment (Zinker, 1977) it was believed that the therapist could repair past damage by giving the client a different experience. This has led many a therapist to engage in "reparative" experimentation involving rocking the client as though he were a baby, feeding the client with a baby bottle and other well-intentioned interventions that can encourage sudden and dangerous regression and dissociation.

One definition of a boundary violation is that the therapist exploits the relationship to meet personal needs (Peterson, 1992). Cooper-White (2001) believes that the "spectre of narcissism" runs through *all* boundary violations including those that do not constitute gross failures in good practice but do or may represent departures from accepted good practice. In other words, disguised as altruism or providing a reparative relationship or general acts of kindness is a desire, not just to be caring, but to be the special carer.

The challenge for the supervisor of humanistic therapists is to help them to differentiate between a conscious desire to be supportive and affirming and an out-of-awareness need to be seen as special and limitlessly loving.

Touch

Maintaining good boundaries is one way of conveying holding without touching. Boundaries help the client to *feel* held without actually *being* held. There is no general agreement amongst humanistic therapists about the use of touch in psychotherapy. Certain gestalt practitioners have gone so far as to propose that a blanket proscription against touch would in itself be unethical in light of the therapeutic value of touch and of the ethical imperative to uphold the welfare of the client (Murray, Pugh & Clance, p. 138). In my own practice I have come to the conclusion that touch, even casual touch, carries as much potential for misunderstanding as it does for healing. I know that some therapists regularly hug their clients when they arrive or as they are leaving. My advice to the practitioner, particularly the practitioner in private practice whose greetings and leave-takings with clients are unlikely to be observed by other colleagues or staff is to err on the side of caution.

Furthermore, in the session itself, if you don't have specific training in the therapeutic or healing use of touch and if your contract with the client does not make explicit that you will use the laying on of hands in your work, don't. I often encounter inexperienced therapists, particularly gestalt therapists, who say that their theory supports bodywork. Indeed it does. But it is possible to work with the body without ever touching the client. This can be done through visualisation and other creative techniques. I would argue that all psychotherapy is bodywork as emotions, memory and imagination are body experiences.

I remember hearing a tape of a session during which a female therapist dealt skilfully and respectfully with a very lonely and schizoid male client's longings around touch. Therapist and client were exploring the limits of their relationship. The client said to the therapist, with anguished frustration in his voice, "But I can't touch you". There followed a silence, after which the therapist replied, "Ah, but you do touch me. I feel very touched by what you say, by the poetry and the passion with which you talk about your life. I *feel* touched by you". This intervention stands in marked contrast to another colleague, a very experienced male therapist, who explained to me that he was exploring working with touch with a very damaged female client because, in his words, "I am the only one she trusts". This kind of rationale is fraught with the possibility that the therapist's own narcissistic edges have been activated in the countertransference and that he is making the decision to touch to satisfy his own need rather than in the interest of the client.

"The forbidden zone?"

In *Sex in the Forbidden Zone* (1991) Rutter makes the point that sexual relations should be taboo in any situation where one person is in the care of another, where there are disparities of power or where expertise is involved or the conferring of qualifications. Sexual relations in such circumstances are, he says, inherently exploitative.

There are all too common sexual misdemeanours that arise from mismanaging both the real and the transferential aspects of the therapeutic relationship. The impulse to act on and sexualise loving feelings toward one's client, however real it feels, needs to be understood as transference and managed accordingly. On the other end of the spectrum some therapists metaphorically run away from the client who falls in love (or hate) with them and avoid these powerful erotic feelings altogether. (See Chapter Four for a fuller discussion of erotic transference).

I have heard it argued by humanistic therapists that sexual relationships with clients are acceptable after a suitable interval. Bob and I take the view that this may be acceptable in some relationships where there is a power differential such as student/teacher or supervisor/ supervisee but it is not true of the relationship between a therapist and a client. Both of us believe that the transferential aspects of those relationships never end and that sexual relationships with former clients, even after many years, will always be on some level abusive.

There was a time when it was reasonable for therapist and client to have social contact after the therapy had ended. A recent complaint that I have been told about involves a set of circumstances that occurred some ten years ago. A client had been in therapy to explore his recent decision to end his marriage and to move in with the woman who had just recently become his lover. Sometime after the therapy had finished he asked the therapist out to lunch as a way of moving forward to a more social relationship and of saying "thank you". The therapist accepted the invitation and she and her client continued to meet occasionally, always instigated by the client. Some time later he rang his former therapist to ask for some emergency sessions on how to approach his wife for a reconciliation, to which the therapist agreed. His lover saw him enter the therapist's house and accused the therapist of having a sexual relationship with him. To make matters worse it turned out that the lover had briefly been a client of the same therapist. It was and continues to be a mess.

Not only does the above example speak to how easily boundaries can become intertwined without the therapist's knowledge but it also shows how, in the client's mind, the therapy had not come to an end. Even though he and his "former" therapist had a casual, social relationship he seemed to hold in his mind the option of resuming the therapy at some later date. The therapist colluded with this by not referring him to someone else for the next piece of work.

Humanistic therapy has grown up in and survived the permissive culture of the 1960s and 70s where making friends with clients and even forming intimate relationships during or after the therapy was not seen as problematic. Humanism has come to acknowledge the power differential inherent in the therapeutic relationship as well as the existence of transference. Nevertheless even now there are people who embark on trainings where transference is still not addressed.

Some years ago a colleague came to me for support with a therapeutic relationship that went badly wrong. The general good feeling and positive intent that characterised the work from the beginning had slipped into a more personal warmth and closeness. My colleague pursued a "friendship" with her client once the work came to an end, even suggesting that the client might want to go into therapy with someone else and giving him a list of therapists. After a short period of having limited social contact the client moved to the same street in an attempt to pursue a more intimate relationship. My colleague applied the brakes but it was too late. As you can imagine things went badly wrong. A "jilted" client became the neighbour from hell.

Bee Springwood, who writes in Chapter Seven of her organisation's journey towards a humanistic system of resolving complaints, wrote to me of her personal experience of being in a stuck place with a client who was unable or unwilling to grow out of a positive attachment. "I work in a reasonably small town and encountered my client in a social situation. I thought that this meant handling a difficult situation by being entirely available to my client, while also not disclosing our relationship, and hiding any needs of my own. If I could supervise myself now, twenty years on, I would have been able to take this back into the work and use our mutual feelings. As it turned out, feeling compelled to give my full attention in a social situation turned my client into something of a stalker".

"Transferential stalking" has evolved into a very serious business for a colleague in a different town. A client who was unwilling to end therapy, engaged her partner to torment the therapist. Over time the partner joined all the social and sporting groups where my colleague met her friends, prompting her withdrawal, bit by bit, from her normal life. No direct threat was issued, but the fear and isolation engendered were effective, and my colleague's hands felt tied by confidentiality. It was several years before she could rebuild a fulfilling and nurturing social life.

Working beyond the metropolis

Working as a therapist in less-than-urban areas carries its own set of difficulties. Bee wrote in another email:

"Early on in my work as a therapist I realised there was a sort of limitation on my actions in the wider world, because clients or potential clients could be watching. I didn't especially want to get drunk in public, or have a messy affair. But I *did* want to exhibit my art work, and perform with a band in public, and it took some soul searching as well as some considered negotiating and fielding of feelings with some clients when I decided I must risk more public exposure for the sake of my own well-being. I have had a client flee an open arts workshop after seeing my name on the list or participants—leaving me no time to negotiate to leave myself—who was later furious that she had no prior warning that I would be there. We worked this through. But doing so required her willingness to recognise me as a human being with a separate life at a time when she still wanted me to be 100% her own. We worked out a way to manage bumping into each other that included taking some shared responsibility for where would each be, and when! Working in a small town I have needed to become skilful about managing boundaries, checking not just social but other possible connections with potential clients. I once had to turn down a client who had the same surname as my dentist".

Even in London in my early life as a therapist, I was plunged into an accidental dual relationship at a dinner party. I had a part in setting this up, as the host had referred a friend to me for therapy some months back and I made the assumption, without being specific about the reasons, that she would not invite us both to the same dinner party. It took some time for me to find a way to exit, without disclosing both my discomfort and need to protect the client as the reason for my departure. Now I always refer clients who are referred to me through friends to someone else.

Money

> *Money is a boundary in the sense of defining the business nature of the therapeutic relationship. This is not love; it's work.* [Gutheil & Gabbard, 1993, p. 192]

There is an apocryphal story about Hahnemann, the founder of homeopathy that, I believe, has relevance to those of us who charge fees directly to our clients. According to Jutte (1999), long before allopathic doctors asked their patients to pay in cash, Hahnemann, whose unorthodox ideas were scorned by the medical establishment, worked solely for cash payments, using a sliding scale to allow for the individual economic circumstances of his patients. He treated the poor for free but, in other cases, he charged very high fees, something that his enemies often used against him. On one occasion, after treating a very wealthy man, Hahnemann explained that his patients paid according to their means. The patient replied that he believed in trading like for like, took out of his wallet a note of high value, passed it under Hahnemann's nose and left the surgery.

Klebanow and Lowenhopf (1991) proposed that there is a conspiracy of silence surrounding the issue of money in the psychotherapy profession. Kruger (1986) saw issues of money as "the last taboo" and believed that as a profession we feel collective shame about charging people to care about them. This is probably more true in the UK because of the welfare state and the expectation of "free" health care. I believe that the collective shame we experience about charging people is also due to us not taking ourselves seriously as a profession. Many people still see psychotherapy as an "alternative" therapy, like homoeopathy and acupuncture. Can we be as certain sure as doctors that our "treatment" will work? Given the inherent degree of uncertainty in any therapeutic relationship how do we justify charging? We struggle between seeing our work as a job or as a vocation.

During a discussion on the "money" day with the first cohort of *"The Seven Deadly Sins?"*[1] it was revealed that less that half the participants were earning their living exclusively from the practice of psychotherapy/counselling. Only 5% were the main breadwinners in their families. This revelation led one of the participants to wonder if psychotherapy was more of a "hobby" than a profession. Many of us experienced a conflict between our need to meet our financial requirements and our desire to "help".

It has been my experience that the therapist's anxiety or lack of clarity about money issues is frequently the starting point for the disintegration of a therapeutic relationship. As a supervisor I notice again and again how the therapist's anxiety over losing people or about scarcity is non-verbally conveyed through not holding the boundary around fees and cancellations. What may seem to the therapist as a kindness to the client may be perceived by the client as not being strong enough or even too needy. This will be a signal to clients whose self-process is fragile that the therapist is vulnerable and may leave the well-meaning and flexible therapist open to attack.

Money is a crucial component of "the frame" in psychotherapy. In addition as a complex economic, social and psychological phenomenon, it has both practical, symbolic and emotional value. Our attitude to money reflects our existential attitude to life.

Trachtman (1999) believes that money as a psychological phenomenon is our projection onto coins, notes, bank accounts and other financial instruments of our beliefs, hopes and fears about who we are, what will happen to us and how we will be treated by self and others. He identifies six possible conditions, which I've slightly adapted here for the British ear, that support the psychological meaning of money: 1) I've got enough money; 2) I haven't got enough money; 3) I've got too much money; 4) They've got enough money; 5) They haven't got enough money; 6) They've got too much money. These are the conditions that mirror our worth in relation to our self and others and are the bases of whether we live our lives from a place of satisfaction, scarcity, guilt, envy and greed.

You might find it interesting to think of a significant expenditure you have undertaken in the last few years (significant does not necessarily mean expensive). What sort of process did you go through to arrive at the decision to spend money on this thing or event or cause? Were there other people involved in or affected by the decision. If so, what was it like to negotiate the outcome? If no one else was involved what was it like arriving at the decision on your own? Looking back at this significant expenditure can you see how influences from your past, particularly your family of origin, affected the outcome? Most importantly, with hindsight, was it worth it? How do you know? What is your earliest memory of money? When you don't have enough money—or if you think you've got too much—how do you feel? What do you do?

When groups of qualified psychotherapists were asked to free-associate to the word "money" the flip-chart looked like this: Security, sense of identity, success, freedom, power, control, autonomy, independence, status, choice, guilt, space, time, responsibility, envy, greed, power, corruption. A second free-association exercise to the question, "What do you do it for if not for the money?" yielded interesting results: to hear stories, to solve puzzles, to heal myself, for more free time, to be more control of my time, to feel important, to feel needed, to be able to take school holidays and, of course, to help others.

Anything that is the container of the projections of our beliefs, hopes and fears is going to be complex to say the least. Add to that our social background and society's beliefs, hopes and fears around class and education and we've got a minefield. Just because we don't consciously think about the significance of money doesn't mean that all this isn't affecting us unconsciously pretty much all of the time.

Can't buy me love

What, then, is the therapist selling? We are indeed in a strange business being far less confident than other professionals that what we are taking money for is actually going to be effective. "Success" in psychotherapy involves the client being able to form a relationship with the therapist in the service of his own healing and more and more people who enter into psychotherapy do so because at some level their ability to relate to others is impaired. No wonder we feel guilty about charging.

I remember a client telling me in no uncertain terms when I invited her to look at something that was uncomfortable for her: "Don't make me do that. I pay you to care for me!" For all sorts of reasons

I couldn't stop thinking about what she had said. "Am I", I wondered, "paid to care?" I thought of a friend who is an anaesthetist. He used to say when his patients asked him why he charged so much just to put them to sleep, "Putting you to sleep I do for free. It's waking you up that is expensive". In that context I came to the conclusion that I am indeed paid to care; I am paid to care for myself. I am reminded of Kohut's (1982) definition of empathy as "a mode of observation attuned to the inner life" (p. 397). Our clients might feel cared for, even loved, but that is not what we are doing. We are trying to "know" the client's inner world so that we can help them to know themselves better and to experience themselves in relationship to others.

Legal tender

Geistwhite (2000, p. 143) sees the actual exchange of the therapist's bill and the client's payment as representing one of the few physical exchanges between client and therapist and as a real-life phenomenon that allows for the expression of conflicts that might, if unexpressed, jeopardise the therapy. He has found that managing fee issues is often difficult for beginning therapists because of feelings of guilt and inadequacy. When no fee is charged and/or the therapist is not paid because he is a trainee the therapist may feel exploited. Furthermore both therapist and client can devalue the therapy and themselves: "You get what you pay for" (p. 144). On a more positive note the absence of a fee can help trainee therapists to ease their discomfort about being inexperienced and facilitate some level of self-acceptance (p. 145).

Herron and Rouslin Welt (1992) believe that the unpaid or badly paid therapist is more likely identify with the client's point of view. In my experience reducing fees in private practice can lead to the client believing that she must be grateful to therapist and gratitude is often the springboard for envy. It can activate other narcissistic edges as well, leading the client who pays no fee or very little to feel special. Even making clear arrangements about money and charging fees commensurate with other colleagues won't keep money out of the frame.

Daniella, a fragile yet flamboyant 35-year-old woman who was struggling with issues of self-esteem, sought counselling in a low-cost clinic and was assigned to one of the more experienced trainees who was in supervision with me. The therapy went well and, when the two-year limit set by the agency was about to be reached, neither the therapist nor I thought it would be right for Daniella to finish. The codes of practice of the agency allowed for the therapist to recontract with the client and to see them privately following their placement. This the therapist did with great care, helping Daniella to manage the change from a more "clinical" setting to private practice. The therapist gave Daniella his "Terms and Conditions" sheet covering such things as payment for cancellations and holidays and the therapy marched on. That is until Daniella had to cancel at short notice because she wasn't feeling well. When she came to her session the following week the therapist, who charged his clients weekly, reminded Daniella that she would have to pay for the missed appointment. She flew into a rage, telling–well, yelling, really–the therapist that this proved that he really didn't care about her and was only doing it for the money and trounced out of the room, never to return.

As we unpicked this unsettling experience in supervision we both realised that in our care to ease Daniella's transition from the clinic (where she paid a very low fee to the receptionist) to private practice (where she paid considerably more to her therapist at the end of each session) we had neglected to attend to how the issue of money and payment would affect the relationship. Daniella had *felt* as though her therapist was seeing her for free at the clinic and that he did so because she was special to him. This was partly true. The therapist had not been paid for his clinic work and Daniella *was* a very engaging and challenging client who took up a good deal of space in the therapist's mind between sessions and in supervision. In hindsight I wish I had supported my supervisee to help Daniella to anticipate how having to pay for missed sessions even if she was ill or had a family emergency would be difficult for her to manage, leaving her feeling as though the therapist didn't really care about her.

Given Daniella's rage-full and dramatic departure and the therapist's residual feelings of anxiety we were both concerned that Daniella might seek to make the therapist "pay" for his mistake. However, despite her challenging behaviour, Daniella did not have a history of leaving and attacking and we consoled ourselves with that knowledge, hoping that she would be able to manage her feelings of rejection and to return to therapy some day. In the next chapter I will discuss a framework for assessing clients who are vulnerable to attack the therapist from outside the therapeutic frame. Daniella, as it has transpired, was not one of them. She *was* able, eighteen months later, to contact her therapist and resume the therapy.

NOTE

1. "The Seven Deadly Sins?–issues in clinical practice and supervision for humanistic and integrative practitioners" is a post-qualification training course that looks at subjects that were un or under-discussed in the original training.

CHAPTER THREE

Assessment and risk-management

Anne Kearns

Since the establishment of national organisations such as the United Kingdom Council for Psychotherapy (UKCP) and the British Association for Counselling and Psychotherapy (BACP) that govern psychotherapy and counsellin g in the UK there has been an on-going discourse about the pros and cons of the professionalisation and regulation of the talking cures. (Totton, 1997; Postle, 1998; 2000). Since the 1990s both organisations have taken an increasing interest monitoring training standards and in defining ethical practice. Whatever your personal beliefs if you are a practitioner working in the UK in the 21st century you are working in a climate that is more and more defined by market forces and social trends. Stigler, an economist, won a Nobel Prize for demonstrating that regulation tends to produce the opposite effect from that which its proponents intended. (Stigler, 1971). A friend tells me that complaints against solicitors doubled in the year after procedures became more user-friendly. In his opinion people are complaining more because they *can* and not because there has been a change in the behaviour of solicitors.

To return to the world of economics there is an old adage that says "When Wall Street sneezes, London catches a cold". This is also relevant to the world of psychotherapy. In 1993 Harris, who is a psychologist and a lawyer, wrote in a series of columns (these were later published as a chapter in 1995) that complaints against therapists were increasing exponentially in the US. Sadly this is also true now in the UK.

I must admit that I was both relieved and delighted to discover Harris's work. This I did at a point in my research when I was feeling pretty low after a week during which I heard of two civil actions that had been taken out against psychotherapists *and* was told by some esteemed colleagues that writing a book like this would just have the effect of scaring people. One told me that she didn't want to know about what was happening because, she said, "If I get frightened I won't be able to work". Let me state emphatically that it is not my intention to alarm, rather I want to us all to be better informed in order to support ourselves better, to be more effective and to know the limits–not just of our competence–but the limits of what is realistically possible to achieve and with whom.

Harris believes that the increase in both disciplinary complaints and litigation against therapists in the US was an indirect result of the "explosion of knowledge" about the roots and treatment of Complex Post-Traumatic Stress Disorder (CPTSD). He also believes that the rise in the number of complaints was due to the number of "victim" support organisations that were established to help people to make complaints against their former therapists. In the UK people who want independent advice about making a complaint against a psychotherapist or counsellor are referred by both UKCP and BACP to Witness, formerly POPAN (Prevention of Professional Abuse Network), an organisation founded by two psychotherapists who were concerned about the stories of "abuse" they were hearing from their clients. Witness now extends its remit to embrace all health and social care relationships.

According to their website they envisage a world where health and social care relationships are free of abusive practice. They provide a helpline and support and advocacy services for victims and survivors of professional abuse, as well as campaigning for improvements in policy law and practice, conducting research and providing education and training. Their aims are to support survivors to seek justice; assist survivors to overcome their experience of abuse; reduce the incidence of abuse; decrease the isolation of survivors and increase the confidence of survivors.

I was unable to get up-to-date statistics from Witness but in 1998/99 the breakdown of the allegations of abuse they received was as follows: 88% emotional abuse, 28% sexual abuse, 6% financial abuse and 3% physical abuse. A spokesperson for Witness told me that around 10% of the calls to their helpline result in further action. He also told me that in the last year (2005/06) something in the area of 25 civil actions had been taken to one law firm alone. Most of these have been settled out of court but at least two are, at the time of writing, moving towards a first hearing in front of a district judge. More alarmingly these claims have been supported by Expert Witness testimony that has been written by a psychotherapist with out discussion with the practitioners involved or access to case or supervision notes. This is indeed alarming.

Whilst I applaud the efforts of Witness and other organisations that fight abuse and help survivors to seek justice my concern is that they may unwittingly *encourage* people to take action against their former therapists as a route to empowerment and healing, rather than supporting them to find other solutions. Furthermore I believe that organisations such as the BACP and the member organisations that make up the federal structure of the UKCP may in their handling of complaints have, also unwittingly, colluded with an unconscious desire for revenge and justice as opposed to healing.

What concerns me about some of the complaints that I have followed is that they don't involve gross professional misconduct such as sexual abuse and financial exploitation but, rather, focus on what the UKCP now calls "minor failures in good practice". Harris saw this trend in the US in the 90s when he noticed that more and more complaints were being brought by former clients who were dissatisfied with the results of their treatment and believed that the therapist "mishandled" their case (p. 249). Moreover he noticed that many of these types of complainants had formal diagnoses on the DSM Axis II (see p. 43) *and* had been victims of serious trauma before coming into therapy, usually physical and sexual abuse.

I have previously published my "map" of fragile self process, looking at a continuum of personality styles (Kearns 2005) in which I understand those clients who fall between the narcissistic and borderline points on the continuum to be people who combine having had inconsistent, abusive or chaotic experiences of parenting as infants with having also experienced painful and abrupt betrayal or rejection later in life involving a third party (losing daddy to mummy in the Oedipal crisis; losing status to a new baby, bullying by a "perfect" sibling, and, often, sexual abuse by a family member, friend or trusted professional). These clients are very difficult to treat in that, due to their histories of abuse and betrayal, they are likely at some point in the therapeutic journey to see the therapist in the transference as abusive and betraying. This often happens *after* they have formed a positive, idealising attachment to the therapist. It is essential in the current climate that practitioners learn to recognise these clients and to put facilitative contracts with the client and consultations with other professionals in place as soon as possible in the therapy. I want to stress that these clients have very troubled and abusive histories and do not come into therapy with the conscious intention of attacking the therapist. However, the relational conditions of the therapy itself are likely to trigger earlier relational states that cause the client to re-enact an earlier trauma by complaining about the therapist.

What I hope to give you in the rest of this chapter is some understanding of why Complex PTSD *is* so complex, of how to recognise clients with Axis II diagnoses and of how to put things into place that can better support the work or onward referral.

A colleague says that something about these clients pushes her into their world. Feeling attracted by their issues she can get drawn in and then, after some time, feel herself wanting to cry, "Whoa!" She describes the need to hold on to the reins from the beginning, even *before* feeling that familiar, "over-involved" feeling.

Complex PTSD

Janet, a contemporary of Freud, noticed that people who had been traumatised became arrested in some way. Freud observed similar phenomena in his patients and, initially, came to the conclusion that their "hysterical" symptoms were caused by having been seduced in childhood, causing them to be "doomed to repeat" the original trauma rather than to remember it. He called this the "repetition compulsion" and based much of his technique on the belief that if his patients could remember the original trauma they would be cured of their symptoms.

Humanistic therapies have their version of Freud's theory. Perls based his gestalt therapy on the concept from gestalt psychology of "unfinished business" meaning that the ego seeks closure and will repeat past experience in order to complete it or "close the gestalt". TA's "racket system" is a model of how people often live in the present as though it were the past. Both of these therapies share with Freud the view that remembering or re-experiencing the past will produce change in the present.

This has not been my experience in my own therapy and it has not been borne out in my clinical practice either. I can think of many clients who had vivid memories of childhood abuse who still lived in the present as though it were the past. van der Kolk (1989) says that clinical experience shows that clients rarely gain mastery over the past by repeating it until it is remembered. This has implications for how we work with what Rothschild (2000) calls Type IIB clients. These differ from what she calls Type IIA clients–people who have been repeatedly traumatised *and* have stable backgrounds and the personal resources that enable them to observe their experience in the here and now. Type IIB clients have also been repeatedly trauma-tised but are not able to distinguish one event from another. They are both overwhelmed and overwhelming and, as a result, have a lot of what Rothschild calls "experiencing self" and very little "observing self". These are the kinds of clients who very quickly develop intense reactions towards the therapist, stemming from idealisation to rage.

Herman (1992) suggested the term Complex PTSD to describe those clients who have been exposed to repeated trauma as opposed to a single traumatic event. These are people who may have endured captivity or torture during times of war or under oppressive regimes, or situations where they were under another's total control such as prostitution, domestic violence or child physical or sexual abuse. The diagnosis of borderline personality disorder is often given to people–particularly women—who were seriously abused as children. Herman (1992), Kroll (1993) and others have written about the treatment implications of working with what Kroll calls PTSD borderlines and I encourage you to familiarise yourself with their thinking when working with this type of client, whatever you want to call them.

The difficulty in helping these clients is that they, according to Herman (p. 138), are particularly resistant to change and are likely to attribute to the therapist many of the same motives as the perpe-trator(s) and to suspect the therapist of exploitative intentions. It is often only through clear contracting and grace that these clients are able to stay in the therapy long enough in order to work through what Herman describes as "complex transference reactions".

Kroll reminds us that these clients are likely to find regular fault with the therapist. Herman (p. 137) says that when the therapist fails to live up to the client's idealized expectations–*as he inevitably will fail*–the patient is often overcome with fury. Because the client feels as though her life depends upon her rescuer (the therapist) she can not afford to be tolerant; there is no room for human error ... *there have to be consequences*. The message is loud and clear. When work-ing with people who have survived childhoods where abuse was common, whose ability to trust anyone has been understandably impaired and who do not have much ability to observe themselves in the world mistakes in the therapy *will* happen.

Kroll reminds us that these clients are likely to find regular fault with the therapist. Herman explains that clients like this will feel rage at people who try to help them and may be driven by the need for revenge. She believes that, out of their awareness, they need to instil in the therapist who disappoints them "the same unbearable condition of terror, helplessness and shame that they themselves have suffered" (p. 138).

Working with people like this requires that therapists pay rigorous attention to what is being evoked in them in the therapeutic relation-ship as well as to their support system (such as supervision, peer con-sultation and the therapist's own therapy) and to boundaries.

Assessment

A careful assessment is our best support. Whilst I don't want to see a generation of therapists who practice defensively and who lose sight of our clients' very real suffering and distress, I *do* want to encourage you to take seriously the experience of others and to sharpen your ability to tell one sort of person, clinically, from another.

One way of doing this is to become familiar with the DSM IV (American Psychiatric Association 1994) multi-axial model of diag-nosis that is, I believe, compatible with humanistic principles and is worth getting to grips with. Please don't let the word "diagnosis" put you off. It means, without all the baggage that has been loaded on to it by decades of being misused to label and control, to discern through knowledge. Please remember that.

Axis I refers to what the client "has". This includes the sort of presenting problems that we see in every-day practice such as depression, anxiety, alcoholism or eating disorders as well as serious mental illnesses like schizophrenia and bi-polar disorder.

Axis II refers to how a client *is* in the world as opposed to what a client *has*. In order for a client to warrant an Axis II "personality disorder" diagnosis they need to meet at least 5 criteria in at least one category. Having said that, all of us have personality styles even though we may not meet the criteria for a full-blown disorder, and each client's way of being in the world and with others is essential to any initial assessment.

There are an increasing number of people seeking therapy who present with no clear Axis I diagnosis but, rather, with feelings of emptiness, relational difficulties, procrastination, low-self esteem, problems managing their anger or complicated relationships with things such as work, food, drugs or alcohol. People with personality disorders can be seen as having interpersonal and behavioural patterns that are limited in range and that are maladaptive. In other words they find themselves doing the same thing or choosing the same kind of person over and over again, even though these 'choices' don't really work for them.

Fragile self-process is *always* a complex and relational process involving another person or internal and external conditions. It can't be reduced to a list of behavioural criteria as 'other' is not fixed, even though our response to "other" may be predictable and habitual. Many of these people show signs of disorder or fragile self-process in certain important or intimate relationships or in private, as in the case of problems with food or other substances, yet may appear to be fairly together to the rest of the world.

Even though the DSM IV divides personality disorders into three "clusters" and 13 categories it's worth noting that all people with personality disorders or fragile self-process have as much in common as they are different. Johnson (1994) sees that all people with personality disorders are united by a very low tolerance for and difficulty in containing a number of affective states: anxiety, frustration, aggression, grief or loss, love or intimacy (p. 14). All rely on more "primitive" defences such as splitting, which is usually manifested by moving very quickly back and forth between extreme views such as idealisation and devaluation, and projection, where what can not be experienced in the self is attributed to someone or something else in the environment. Another common defence is merging with another in order to achieve a feeling of oneness, the loss of which is experienced by people with more borderline and narcissistic defences as annihilating.

The dynamics of this feeling of merging are the same as the dynamics of empathy: projection and identification. The client imagines that she and the therapist are alike; she also projects that she is the most important person in the therapist's world *and* that the therapist will be the one to save her from her by now internalised persecutor. As long as this idealised state is maintained all may appear to go well and the client does not have to experience her "real" feelings of rage and envy alongside love and dependence. In an ideal world the client will be helped to gradually contain the reality of the therapist's separate feelings, thoughts and experience. When this happens suddenly due to elements from outside of the therapy or "real life" breaking the frame (another client arriving early, a family member greeting the client, the therapist's illness or bereavement or even a planned holiday) the client may be plunged into a despairing and attacking negative transference.

Axis III refers to any medical conditions that may impact on the overall picture such as any chronic physical illness or pain, such as a bad back. Clients with a CPTSD presentation often have accompanying somatisation that shows itself in eczema, herpes, psoriasis, asthma and chronic fatigue or pain.

Axis IV, "psycho-social stressors", looks at the events in the clients life, usually in the recent past, that have had an impact on them as well as at the current picture such as a promotion at work, the birth of a child or the death or someone close to them. I like to use this axis to look at the level of the client's psycho-social support in order to assess if she has activities or people in her life that give her meaning or that pull her down as this will impact the direction of the therapy. A client who has very little outside support may rely too heavily on the therapist or may find therapy too challenging.

Axis V or "global assessment of functioning" asks the question: given all of the above how is this person doing? For example, someone who has moved to a new country, developed a back problem and experienced a bereavement all in the same year who is a little depressed is coping fairly well.

If I got to have a crack at rewriting the DSM I would add one further axis–let's call it Axis VI—that would make room in the diagnostic picture for the therapist's reactions to the client. I want to challenge humanistic practitioners to find ways of accepting and working with "unconscious" material in ways that may at first feel at odds with their humanistic principles. I have previously published (Kearns, 2005) a sort of "map" that I devised for myself and for my supervisees that seeks to divide people into categories in order to emphasize the commonality of human experience as well as to emphasize that there *are* differences between us and that we feel and think and behave with some people differently than we feel and think and behave with others. I believe along with countless others that these feelings and thoughts and behaviours, when occurring in a boundaried therapeutic relationship, are essential sources of information about the client's relational history, her current relational challenges and the anticipated direction of the therapy. I believe that we need to enter fully into those thoughts and feelings in an internal dialogue and in supervision in order to see them as something the client is telling us that she has not got the words to say. I think it was Freud who described the analyst as a finely-tuned telephone receiver. I like to think of myself as getting "signals" from my clients through the airwaves that I need somehow to turn into a human voice. I have found my own on-going psychotherapy an invaluable support in learning to distinguish between what belongs to me alone and what is information about the client.

Gretl[1]

Gretl is 45 and is going through an acrimonious divorce from her husband of 20 years. She does not work outside the home due to repetitive strain injury that keeps her from being able to use a keyboard. She and her husband have three children–two daughters and a son and are involved in a custody battle over the youngest son who is 13. Gretl describes herself as "having woken up at 40". She tells the story of attending a personal development weekend with a friend and realising that she had been living her life since the age of 13 in denial of having been sexually abused by her older brother every time he came home from university and they were alone in the house. After university he moved to Australia following a year of travelling and she has had very little contact with him since. She reports with some pride that, although she has never told her parents about the abuse, she *has* succeeded in becoming the "favourite child", discouraging her parents from visiting her brother and his family.

Gretl's husband left the family home three years ago following her continuing allegations that he had "behaved inappropriately" with their youngest daughter. The daughter denies this but Gretl believes that she is in denial like she was. A year after her husband moved out a young woman was murdered in a nearby village. After hearing the details of the murder and the police's profile of the murderer Gretl went to the police and told them that she believed her husband could be the person they were looking for. They did not take their inquiries further and Gretl believes that the police are protecting her husband, who is a respected member of the community and active in charity work through the Rotary Club. She wrote to the chief constable saying that the police's failure to investigate was making her suicidal and received a letter suggesting she seek counselling. When questioned about the suicide by her therapist Gretl said that she was not really suicidal but wanted to make them pay attention.

Gretl consults tarot cards when she has an important decision to make or to help her to "know what's coming." She believes she has a special gift for intuition and for helping others and finds it difficult to understand why she was "dropped" from the three-year diploma course that she attended after the first year. She describes a social life that consists mostly of contact with other women she has met in personal development groups, having had a particularly intense involvement with one of them with whom she has recently fallen out. She drinks occasionally, does not use drugs and has recently come to believe that some of her non-specific difficulties with what she calls stress are due to food intolerances. She no longer eats wheat or dairy or sugar and regularly consults alternative practitioners such as nutritionists and homeopaths seeking diets and "remedies" to give her more energy. Recently a cranial osteopath suggested to her that she might be putting too much emphasis on finding a "cure" for what is just part of being alive. Gretl is enraged by this and asks the therapist if that is what she believes. The therapist felt put on the spot, as though any answer would be the "wrong" answer.

Gretl has had a year of counselling and describes her former counsellor as having been inadequate in various ways. When asked to elaborate on "how" Gretl is vague but says she never felt *really* listened to.

My supervisee feels warmly disposed towards Gretl and looks forward to working with her. I feel increasingly anxious and notice that my heart is beating faster than usual. I ask her how she sees the work with Gretl progressing. She replies that Gretl needs to be taken seriously and to have support during a difficult time. I ask her what she makes of Gretl's remarks about her previous counsellor and she seems startled. I persist. She replies, "If I'm honest I feel a bit superior to her–like *I* will succeed where *she* has failed". I wonder aloud about an initial diagnostic hypothesis.

Let's look at Gretl using the DSM five-axis system in a slightly different order than the people who designed it intended, adding a sixth axis that holds the therapist's–and supervisor's–countertransference.

Axis I

None. Gretl sees herself as a "little stressed". She sleeps well and eats well within her rather limited range of choices. She is not suicidal.

Axis III

None. Gretl's food intolerances are self-diagnosed and probably form part of her support system and make her feel special and in control.

Axis IV

Gretl's significant stressors include an acrimonious divorce, recovered memories of sexual abuse, not having her allegations taken seriously by the police and being dropped from her counselling course.

Gretl's support system includes feeling that she is her parents' favourite child, her friends from her personal development network, various alternative practitioners, and her ability to feel in control through her diet and reliance on tarot cards to predict the future.

Axis V

Given all of the above Gretl seems to be doing pretty well. Or is she? The picture changes when be bring in Axes II and "VI".

Axis II

People let Gretl down. She has intense involvements with some people and some of her relationships end badly or without her understanding why. She has made serious allegations about her soon to be ex-husband and has involved her daughter in this against her wishes. She has used the threat of suicide to manipulate others. Her difficulties with "stress" may suggest poor frustration tolerance, particularly when other people don't see things her way. She has succeeded in her mind in becoming her parents' favourite child.

"Axis VI"

The therapist feels warm and protective towards Gretl, even to the point of believing that she will succeed where others have failed. She also admits to having felt put on the spot and feeling some anxiety about getting it wrong. The supervisor could feel her heart beating faster than usual and is also aware of feelings of dread.

I want to expand to how I use what is being evoked in me as a supervisor to support the therapist in anticipating the direction of the therapy. It has been my experience that certain affective and somatic states are evoked in me as a supervisor in order for me to be able to begin to hold and to metabolise that which the therapist cannot yet bear. The process of using these feeling states to support the therapist can be tricky, particularly with humanistic therapists who like to think the best of people and who tend to shy away from their less-than-positive reactions to their clients. In the example above my feelings of anxiety and dread led me to hypothesize that Gretl has both borderline and narcissistic features to her personality. The therapist's belief that *she* would succeed where others have failed supported my hypothesis. In my experience this activation of the redeemer archetype usually means that there is a narcissistic process at work and that the therapist may be putting herself at risk.

Harris has written that the four highest risk situations for a therapist are (1) working with a client who has a primary diagnosis on Axis II *and* has been–and I would add claims to have been–the victim of serious trauma in childhood or adolescence, particularly physical or sexual abuse; (2) working with a potentially violent or suicidal client; (3) working with someone who is involved in a contested divorce or custody case; and (4) working in a therapeutic relationship in which there is an unusually rapid or intense transference and countertransference (p. 251). According to these criteria Gretl is a very risky client. She is not deliberately malicious but has, we can assume, experienced repeated relational trauma and *will* find a way to relive that trauma with the therapist. This is the kind of client who may, when her feelings of oneness with the therapist are shattered by the therapist's even gentle challenge or holding a different point of view or when feeling let down by the therapist when the therapist's life impinges on the work in some way or even when the therapy has come to an end and she doesn't feel that much better than before, take a complaint out against the therapist finding fault with elements of the therapeutic relationship that a different client might have seen as par for the course in any relationship.

When I read the substance of various complaints against psychotherapists the "clues" were always there from the beginning. Therapists need to learn to listen for clues, whilst at the same time remaining open to the client's relational strivings. Listening for clues necessarily entails more attention to unconscious or nonverbal material and less exclusive emphasis given to "being real" in the here and now encounter. Verbal clues I have noticed involve the client talking in veiled terms about wanting to "destroy someone" or to make someone "pay" for what they've done. This often takes the form of an intractable disagreement with a family member, boss or another helping professional. Kroll says that these clients have "a drivenness" to prove the accuracy of a distorted worldview and to re-play old painful experiences in the therapeutic relationship rather than look at process and pattern (p. 160). This leads them to develop an often intractable negative transference that, if not held and worked through, may get played out on a wider stage in the form of a complaint or civil action.

How do people get like this?

Research done by Schore (1994; 2001) and others has confirmed many theories about what makes people tick, particularly attachment theory. It is generally accepted that people with histories of secure attachment (Bowlby, 1969) respond to and recover from trauma better than the rest of us. This is because trauma commonly brings about a partial and temporary collapse of the ability to regulate emotion and of the *mentalising capacity* (Fonagy & Target, 1977). This basically refers to our ability to reflect on our own and other's experience. If someone is about to run you over in the street you don't spend a second imagining what it must be like to be so stressed and aggressive. You jump out of the way. And with any luck you pick yourself up and walk on, shaken. Only later might you discover that you've scraped your knee. And you'll tell someone how some idiot nearly killed you, feeling self-righteous maybe but not in the least bit self-reflective or empathic. So far so good. The next time you cross the road you will, no doubt, be a bit more vigilant and you'll eventually come to believe that, even though the bus driver may in fact be an idiot, he probably wasn't out to get you that day.

People with complicated or impaired attachment histories can't do this. After the same type of encounter with the same idiot bus driver they may become fixated on what they did to provoke or to deserve the incident and will punish themselves over and over again in their minds for not having been watching where they were going. Or they might come to see all buses as potential predators and anxiously avoid them. Some might even believe that the bus driver *was* trying to kill them. I had a client who tried to get London Transport to write to him to apologise on behalf of one of their drivers, even though my client could not describe the driver in any way that he could be identified and wasn't sure whether it was a number 45 or 236. These are all failures of the mentalising function. We are not born with the capacity for emotional regulation and we don't get good at it without a primary caregiver who can read and respond to our emotional signals, moment to moment. Our past experiences with our primary caregiver–usually mother–form "internal working models" (Bowlby, 1973) which form the basis of how we relate to ourselves and others in times of stress. No mother or primary caregiver can be perfectly attuned to her baby. To help with the reality of having to soothe themselves infants need to develop the capacity to conjure up a good enough, soothing mother or the feelings associated with mother when she is not around or when she gets it wrong.

You may be familiar with Ainsworth's (1978) "Strange Situation" experiments in which infants who were playing in a room occupied also by their mother and a stranger were left alone with the stranger for a brief while and then mother returned. Infants who had "secure" attachments to mother played and explored the room contentedly in her presence, became anxious when left alone with the stranger and sought comfort from and were soon reassured by mother when she returned. Those infants who appeared to be less anxious when left with the stranger and who also did not appear to seek comfort from mother when she returned were termed "anxious/avoidant". Others, termed "anxious/resistant" were limited in their ability to play and explore when mother was present. They were highly distressed by her absence but were not comforted by her return and appeared to reject mother's attempts to soothe them. The anxious/avoidant children shut down on their emotions under stress while the anxious/resistant children loudly expressed their distress, seeming desperate for contact on the one hand and actively dismissing it on the other.

A fourth group of infants fell into the "disorganised/disoriented" category. These were the children who froze or engaged in repetitive movement such as hand-clapping or, more distressingly, head-banging when mother left the room which they continued well after she returned. Mother was someone who was feared as well as a source of comfort. These children were thought to have had a history of severe neglect or physical or sexual abuse.

In a ten year study of the developing brain Schore (1994) has made discoveries that prove what some schools of psychotherapy have hypothesised all along: that we are motivated by impulses that are unconscious or out of awareness, that these impulses are relational and that injuries in the process of attachment between infant and mother can only be healed face to face, right brain to right brain. The human brain grows and changes in relationship with another brain.

The essential task of the first year of life is the creation of a secure attachment bond between the infant and the primary caregiver. An abusive caregiver not only plays less with her infant but also induces traumatic states of enduring negative affect. She is inaccessible or unreliable in times of stress. Instead of soothing her baby she induces extreme levels of stimulation and arousal and, because she provides little or no interactive repair the infant's intense negative states last for long periods of time. If the infant has to endure highly charged negative emotional states biochemical changes will take place it its developing brain. The developing brain deals with these unbearable anxieties through the mechanisms of hyperarousal and dissociation or, what Putnam (1997) calls, "the escape when there is no escape". Because a child inevitably seeks a parent when distressed or frightened, any parental behaviour that directly distresses or alarms the child places him in an "irresolvable paradox" in which he can neither approach the parent, shift his attention elsewhere or run away. (Schore, 2001; Main & Solomon, 1986).

Even though Gretl's "story" does not refer to her early childhood we can imagine that her early attachments were less than secure. We arrive at this hypothesis because of how she sees others–in this case her husband–as abusers, even murderers, with very little "evidence". Her reliance on tarot cards is evidence of magical thinking and her false allegations and suicidal threats show that she has little ability to imagine how others might be impacted by her actions. My and my supervisee's countertransference are further indicators. She felt like she could rescue Gretl at the same time feeling like she was going to get it wrong. I felt afraid and full of dread.

What support do we need to put in place?

I was discussing the current situation around the increase in ethical complaints with a colleague who is a barrister who was himself subject to, what he described as, a "malicious" complaint. He said that he tells his pupils to get everything in writing. Everything. In the US the concept of "informed consent" means that a client has given consent to the treatment or the course of action based on having been informed about possible risks and anticipated difficulties. In the UK the courts rely on sufficient consent, employing the Bolam Principle (1957), which states that a "doctor" is not negligent if he acts in accordance with a practice that is accepted at the time as reasonable by a body of other practitioners, even though other "doctors" might adopt a different practice. This leaves more leeway than the law in the US for the practitioner to use reasonable judgement about what is best practice.

For the purpose of "risk management" and to protect both the client and the therapist, particularly when working with the sort of challenging client described above, the principle of informed consent should mean that the ground rules of the therapy as well as its potential risks and benefits should be given to the client at the start of any treatment contract in writing. This should include information about length and frequency of sessions, payment and cancellation arrangements, holidays, illness, confidentiality, discussions with third parties such as supervisors, other colleagues and other medical practitioners such as the GP and the use of "case" material for training or research purposes. This should include the taping of sessions (For a sample "Terms and Conditions" see appendix I).

Because these clients are likely to have difficulties with the boundaries of the therapeutic relationships it is essential to be specific about contact outside of the therapy session. Some therapists mention in their "Terms and Conditions" that they will charge pro rata for phone calls that involve more than changing an appointment and for reading letters or emails or reports from the client or from other professionals. They also charge for writing letters to others who may be involved in the treatment such as the GP or a psychiatrist. This does not come from a place of greed or uncaring but from a recognised need to protect themselves from giving too much, thus making themselves less available for the work.

Those therapists who practice from home need also to explain in their "Terms and Conditions" that reasonable care will be taken to keep the therapy space free from interruptions such as noise from other people living in or using the premises, as well as from unwelcome intrusions from workmen and people making deliveries, but that sometimes these will be unavoidable. One of my colleagues, who works with more than one client who is sensitive to intrusion, leaves a note on the front door asking deliverymen and other trades people not to ring the doorbell during certain hours but this does not always work. On one occasion the bell rang repeatedly and he asked his client if she wanted him to go and ask the person to stop. The client said yes. When the therapist returned the client was in a terrible state, saying that she was less important than the delivery that the therapist had been expecting. The therapist was intrigued because he had not said that he *had* been expecting a delivery. In fact he was not. He wondered aloud if his leaving the therapy room for less than a minute had awakened in the client her feelings about mother having left her for an important "delivery" when her brother was born. Although the client seemed to feel soothed by this hunch the incident plunged her into a negative transference from which the therapeutic relationship never recovered, however much the therapist tried to use what happened as an opportunity for relational repair.

Rothschild (2000) says that conflict and feelings of betrayal are inevitable in work with these clients and *must be worked through*. In other words, the inevitable ruptures in the therapeutic relationship must be followed by a period of relational repair. Otherwise the therapy will be used as simply a replay of past relational trauma. Both Rothschild and Herman say that these clients *must* be helped to anticipate that ruptures will happen and to commit to hanging in there during very difficult times. Helping the client to anticipate the difficulties she might encounter along the way could be seen as helping someone whose observing self is under-developed to be cognitively prepared for what might be emotionally overwhelming. As you can see from the example above an apparently benign interruption proved to be too much for the client to hold and for the therapist to help her to work through.

I believe that it is essential not only to help the client to anticipate how everyday life might intrude unhelpfully into the therapy but to let her know as close as possible to the outset of therapy that her life story may contain elements that will cause her along the way to experience times when she will see the therapist as uncaring or withholding or, even, abusive and that it will be important to agree to stay in the relationship to work this through, rather than to leave. Some therapists tell their clients that, after a brief assessment period, they will together make a written agreement that flags up some of the likely relational hurdles that they will encounter along the way (See Chapter Five for an example of this).

Supervision, supervision and more supervision

Because of the intense countertransference reactions that are part and parcel of work with this client group the therapist needs more support than ever. In addition to regular supervision with someone who is experienced in working with clients like this the therapist will also need to set up a peer network consisting of other therapists who are willing to be rung or emailed for support along the way if the supervisor is not available or even if he is. I and others have found personal therapy essential in order to help to separate what belongs to the therapist from what belongs to the client in order to use what is being evoked by the client effectively rather than reactively or defensively. These clients will be constantly looking for non-verbal clues that the therapist is able to hold and metabolise what they can not yet bear and the therapist's own therapy is a good "insurance policy" against stepping into the countertransference as opposed to containing the client's intense emotional reactions.

The therapist on both an unconscious and conscious level must act as an interactive monitor and regulator of the client's dysregulated affective states. (Siegel, 1999, p. 299). The key to this is the therapist's ability to tolerate uncertainty, allow protest, not just hear but *feel* despair and hold the client at moments of explosive rage as well as at moments of implosive collapse and withdrawal. This involves the therapist being able to tolerate intense and enduring negative affect states such as shame, hopelessness and helplessness.

I want to say something here about envy. I have written earlier (Kearns, 2005) that clients will, by nature of the therapeutic relationship and the reasons for entering into it, see the therapist as possessing something they do not. At some level they believe they need the therapist in order to "fix" something that they cannot fix on their own. They may see their therapist as possessing qualities that they believe they lack or they may simply believe we have the answers to their questions. A client coming to therapy is admitting that she needs help from a professional, which immediately puts her in the "weaker" position, no matter how much the therapist believes in co-creation, horizontality, or any of the other euphemisms we use to gloss over the real and transferential power imbalance in the therapeutic relationship.

The envious person projects her sense of inferiority or badness on to the other and then sees "other" as being superior, good and withholding. She then sets about attacking the what she projects on to "other", destroying the good so that both feel depleted. This is particularly true of the sort of client we are discussing in this chapter. As I helped Gretl's therapist explore her countertransference she remembered that Gretl's first remark on entering the therapist's home and walking through the front hallway to the therapy room was, "Well, it's alright for some!" The therapist chose to ignore this at the time but we discussed how she would need to remember that Gretl, with her history of abuse and neglect (remember she was sexually abused by her brother when her parents were away) would be likely to lead her to make envious attacks on the therapist and might also evoke the therapist's envy.

Here's how it works. People who have been neglected or abused or otherwise betrayed develop various defences to cope with their unbearable feelings. Often they come to believe that "everyone else" has something that they haven't got. This defence against feeling so alone may take the form of attacking the therapist's home or developing fantasies about the therapist's life. These will include that the therapist has a perfect life and perfect family. However much our training may support us being open about our marital or relationship status, children and pets telling this type of client about our private life or showing affection for a pet in the client's presence *will* evoke envy, just like the therapist who went to ask someone to stop ringing the doorbell evoked envy. Gomez (1997) reminds us that for clients with Oedipal phase issues (see Chapter Four) to be "only a client" feels unbearable; the thought of other clients, or worse still, those people whom the therapist or counsellor sees because she wants to, not because she is "paid" to, may arouse fury and mortification that may be complicated by earlier developmental disturbance (p. 186). Where self-disclosure is involved (see Chapter Two) with these very damaged and challenging clients less is more.

The therapist's envy may also be evoked, particularly if she becomes over-identified with the "rescuer" and feels bled dry or burnt out. As much as the client may seem to need rescuing she will be keenly attuned to the therapist's vulnerability and is likely to respond with an attack on the therapist if the therapist is not resourced. However tempting it might be to give the extra bit to these clients don't do it. The client will not be grateful for this; on the contrary the more the therapist is seen as the one who is endlessly giving and who will "save" the client from her troubled past the more likely it is that the therapist will fall from grace and be attacked. I discussed this eventuality with Gretl's therapist who agreed to support herself with regular personal therapy. She found it hard to see how her own envy could play a part in the dynamics of the relationship until she realised that Gretl was able to live and support three children without having to work outside the home, whilst the therapist, who had no children but a big mortgage, felt the constant pressure of work.

Record keeping

Whereas there is no legal requirement for counsellors and psychotherapists to keep notes of the work, many professional organisations have a requirement for the therapist to keep records. My advice here is based on the experience of others and is not intended to be legal advice. I can say that I know of precedent where a therapist was asked by the Information Commissioner to release his case notes to a client on the grounds that they were "medical records". He argued successfully that he did not keep case notes *per se* but rather used his notes of his discussions with his supervisor and other colleagues to record his memory and thoughts about the work. As his "supervision notes" were seen to be notes of a discussion with a third party, they were not considered medical records and he was not required to release them to the client. I recommend to my supervisees that they keep minimum records of the client's contact details, history and presenting problem on a formal "intake sheet" and keep "records" of the client's attendance in their diaries or elsewhere. I also recommend that they keep on file a signed copy of the "Terms and Conditions" as well as any other contracts that are made with the client in the course of the therapy. Supervision notes and other private reflections need to be kept separately and be written so as not to identify anyone other than the therapist and members of the therapist's support network.

Familiarise yourself with your codes of ethics

Although the BACP has implemented an ethical framework in an effort to move away from "rule-based" ethics most UKCP member organisations have lengthy codes of ethics and practice. In Chapter One we saw that a significant number of experienced and ethical therapists could not say, hand on heart, that they had really assimilated chapter and verse of their codes of ethics. It also emerged that, particularly for those who had been working for some years since qualifying in one humanistic discipline, their practice was not entirely consistent with humanistic principles.

In the current climate that shows such an increase in ethical complaints and civil actions I would recommend therapists who work with the sort of client we have been discussing to set up for themselves regular ethical review. This means informing a member of your ethics committee that you are working with a particularly troubled and challenging client the moment you realise that this is so and asking them to have an informal discussion with you, say every six months or so, to review the work. I would like to see this become standard practice.

Elkind (1992) has written that the profession of psychotherapy has not recognized that areas of what she calls, "primary vulnerabilities" endure and recur through the life of every client as well as every therapist and that problematic interactions in the therapeutic relationship can stem from the primary vulnerability of the therapist as well as that of the client. She called for therapists to be open to bringing in a consultant to the relationship when it hits an impasse or a rupture, rather than just talking to a supervisor about their difficulties. Such a consultant would either help to resolve the impasse in the therapeutic relationship or to bring it to a fruitful termination. I think this is an idea worth considering in order to reduce the therapist's irrational fear of scrutiny and to protect both the therapist and the client from the trauma of going through a formal complaints procedure.

Onward referral

A colleague who has been subject to what amounts to harassment from a former client likes to relieve the tension when discussing the latest development by quoting Rick from the film "Casablanca" who said of the Ingrid Bergman character: "Of all the gin joints in all the towns in all the world she had to walk into mine!"

I would like to see therapists in the UK take a more robust approach to onward referral. Referring a client on is not an admission of incompetence of failure. Neither should it give a message to the client that she is too difficult. As professionals we have the right to say we don't want to work with someone. Only we can know what our practice can bear. We have a commitment to ourselves and to our other clients not to take on too much. The sort of client that we have been discussing often has a well-developed sense of entitlement. Just because they want therapy doesn't mean that they are ready for it or that you have to be the one to give it to them (For a fuller account of a therapist's struggle with onward referral see Chapter Six).

NOTE

1. "Gretl" is a composite based on the history, presenting problems and personality styles of the clients who took out formal complaints and / or civil actions against the practitioners who contributed to my doctoral research as well as on my clinical experience.

CHAPTER FOUR

Love and hate in the in-between

Anne Kearns and Steven B. Smith

B oth of us have been trained in and are informed by both humanistic and psychoanalytic theories. Our grounding in the humanistic tradition leads us to value the human qualities of clinical relating that research has shown to be essential to a successful therapeutic outcome (Lambert, 1992); the psychoanalytic tradition, particularly where it was developed by the British object relations theorists, supports us in linking child development to adult experience and in learning to listen to communications from our clients that are outside of their awareness.

One of the assumptions that informs our work as integrative psychotherapists and as supervisors is that being able to "read" and process transference–or the client's mostly non-verbal communication of archaic experience—is essential to a successful therapeutic outcome. We feel concerned when we meet humanistic therapists who say that they don't work with the transference. This is nonsense. *All* therapists work with transference. It is in the field of any relationship, particularly ones in which there is a power differential. Humanistic therapists work with the transference differently from more psycho-dynamically trained therapists in that they name, observe and use it rather than primarily interpret it. We want to help the reader to explore the non-verbal and somatic realms of the therapeutic encounter in order to be better supported to work with powerful emotion, particularly when it becomes sexualised.

As we prepared for writing this chapter together we were reminded of the stereotypical image of the "angry young man" tattoed with the words "love" and "hate" across his knuckles–one word for each hand. We imagine that these short, emblazoned words hold powerful resonances of excitement and fear for many of us. We also wondered how our families of origin facilitated these primary emotions either by supporting us to listen and dialogue with these facets of ourselves or to suppress them? As we pondered out childhood experience we began to draw an inquisitive parallel with our humanistic training institutes. As counsellors and psychotherapists trained within the "third force psychology" (Maslow, 1968) of the humanistic movement have we, we wondered, been prepared to deal with love and hate in the clinical encounter, both our own and that of our clients? To begin to answer these questions we want briefly to review the initial responses of the "first force psychology" of the psychoanalytic movement to love and hate.

Love and hate in the psychoanalytic literature

In the history of psychotherapy the powerful emotions of love and hate have been explored mainly within the psychoanalytic tradition, beginning with Freud. In 1930 he looked at the major challenges facing humanity in terms of our propensity towards destruction and explored the conflict between "eros" or the life instinct and "thanatos" or the death instinct. The former emphasises growth and creativity and the latter hate and destruction towards self and others.

Klein was the next to explore the role of love and hate developmentally and as it arose in treatment. She made sense of these emotions within her concept (Klein, 1945) of the "paranoid-schizoid position", which occurs when the child is unable to cope when mother has failed to meet his needs. In order to manage his contradictory feelings of love and hate he splits his internal image of mother into good and bad parts. He fears retaliation for his hateful feelings–this is the paranoid bit—and becomes withdrawn (the schizoid bit). Eventually from 6 months onwards he comes to the realisation that the mother he has hated and loved are one and the same person and this leads the child into the "depressive position". In this position the child begins to appreciate the mother as both good and bad, which helps him to manage the good and bad in others and within himself. This leads to what is known as object constancy: a sense of consistency, coherence and continuity of the self and other over time.

Bion (1962), in developing Klein's theory, warned that responding to the patient's feelings of love and hate in the in-between amounted to nothing more than emotional gratification. He termed these ways of responding the "L"-Link (loving and being loved) and "H""-Link (hating and being hated) respectively. Rather, he argued, it was important for the analyst to work with the "K"-Link (knowledge), which is the task of knowing and being known. This, he believed, would restructure the intra-psychic (internal relationship with the self) world of the patient and such knowledge would empower the patient to respond and manage his love and hate in more satisfying rather than destructive ways. Love and hate as they emerged in the clinical encounter were feelings to be analysed on an intra-psychic and not on an inter-personal level.

Subsequent object relations writers (Fairbairn, 1951; Winnicott, 1965; Bollas, 1987) and further inter-subjective developments (Kohut, 1977; Stolorow & Atwood, 1979) within the psychoanalytic fold would depart from this "one-person psychology" (the patient receiving analysis) to a two person dyad that mirrors the mother-child dyad. In essence the patient no longer just received analysis but became the "analytic-child", an active participant working with the analyst (analytic-parent) in a "two-person psychology".

Humanistic "Two-person psychology"

Of course the humanistic movement has always championed a two-person psychological approach to therapy working with the in-between (the interpersonal) to foster change, growth and healing. It is within this tradition that we stand as integrative psychotherapists prizing the relational, reciprocal and co-created contact between therapist and client to engender psychological (intra-psychic or internal) change and restructuring. It is also within this relational and inter-personal approach that we want to explore love and hate and to support good practice in dealing with these emotions in the in-between.

As we further reflect upon love and hate within the humanistic tradition we maintain that our primary focus on process and the here-and now seems either to drive sex too much to the foreground, as in the case of one therapist who responded immediately in the affirmative when her client asked her if she fancied him; or under-ground altogether as in the case of another therapist who, when reg-ularly brought dreams containing reasonably obvious erotic signals from the client ("I keep dreaming about eating sausages and eggs with you") wondered if the client was feeling fed by her warmth and acceptance.

If we reflect on the first therapist's quick and honest response of, "Of course I do. You are an extremely attractive man", to the client's question, "Do you fancy me?", what, we wonder, would she have said were the client not extremely attractive. We arrived at the con-clusion that answering "yes" or "no" to questions like, "Do you find me attractive?" or "Do you love me?" probably won't move the ther-apy forward either way as the client may either feel unhelpfully spe-cial or hopeful or rejected or crushed.

Although humanistic psychotherapies are predominantly American in origin they stem from the European existentialist tradi-tion. Tudor and Worrall (2006) remind us that Americans such as Rogers who identified with existentialist thinking rendered it more optimistic and pragmatic than in had been in Europe. Rogers and Maslow and Perls drew from a shared, elevated view of human nature that is positive, wholesome and morally good. Humanistic therapies emphasize freedom, authenticity and choice overlooking the reality that life ends in death and that meaning-making does not necessarily lead to happiness. It is our belief that this view with its inherent preference for a positive therapeutic experience and out-come for both client and therapist unwittingly relegates erotic and hateful clinical material into the shadows. We want to expose this distortion of humanistic psychotherapy as a kind of false, plastic romanticism. We both agree and maintain that Rogers' (1951) con-cepts of empathy, unconditional positive regard and congruence are not about gratifying a client's longing to be experienced and treated in the way they would like to be related to now or how they longed to be related to by their parents as children. Rather, we agree more with Kohut's (1977) idea of working with the client's developmental traumas and deficits where the role of the therapist is to mirror back to the client with understanding and empathy how they are authentically experienced in the moment. In this way, through the non-judgemental and non-shaming mirroring of the therapist the client begins to experience herself more deeply and to develop a deeper and broader picture of herself, containing both light and dark, good and bad which will help her to manage the ups and down of emotional life and relating.

Anne has written earlier (Kearns, 2005) of her concern about the assumption that humanistic therapists must have positive *feelings* towards as well as positive *regard* for their clients. She remembers the expression on the face of a newly qualified therapist when she told her that she found one particular client very hard to like. The therapist looked both relieved and anxious and said, "I didn't know we were allowed not to like our clients." This therapist now has come to trust that it is often in her more unsavoury responses to her client that the sources of the client's injuries are discovered and through which the therapist's ability to feel empathy for and hold the client emerges.

The purpose of this chapter is to retrieve and champion love and hate through journeying into the darker or shadow side of the experience of these intense emotions in the clinical setting. By doing so, we hope to equip humanistic practitioners with a deeper working knowledge of transferential and counter-transferential love and hate. We believe that the client's love and hate are always present–even by their apparent absence–in the therapy and that, to a large extent, the capacity of the therapist to recognise this will be dependent on the therapist's relationship with his or her own sexuality and aggression.

We agree with Mann (1997) that erotic transference needs to be seen in the context of love and hate and not narrowly in terms of sex: psychotherapy *is* an erotic relationship! However, we do appreciate that for many of us to be on the receiving end of erotic transference can be threatening. Likewise hateful feelings can be disturbing and frightening. This is no less so when we as therapists experience heightened erotic and hateful feelings towards our clients. It is interesting to note that successful sex workers are extremely clear about their boundaries–or do's and don'ts–in order to make a living by satisfying their clients *and* to keep themselves safe. In a sense we hope to theoretically and clinically draw out the general "do's and don'ts" for working with love and hate as humanistic psychotherapists.

Personal and professional reflections

(AK) I was talking this morning with a colleague who consults me for supervision once a month in a group of other colleagues. She was talking about a relationship with a male client who had been expressing his loving and sexual feelings for her for some time. I noticed that she seemed particularly tired. She replied, after a deep and reflective sigh, "I'm tired of being careful". For the rest of the day we five women–interestingly the 2 men didn't turn up that day–focussed on our fear about dealing with sexual feelings, questions and fantasies in the consulting room. The consensus was that it was less challenging to "talk about sex" when the client is talking about having or wanting to have sex with someone else (or even with himself). One of the participants said, "It's ok as long as sex lives on the other side of the room. Once it comes in my direction I feel like I've hit a wall of incest".

This therapist had an integrative training that included various psychodynamic approaches. The other therapists were trained in humanistic approaches, which they described as having no theory about psycho-sexual development or erotic transference and no language to support "sexual" interventions. One, trained in person-centred and TA therapy, said that until today she always thought it was good enough to say that her code of ethics forbade her to have sex with clients if the client brought that possibility into the room. As we explored this further the therapist became aware that she felt a certain amount of shame at not feeling any theoretical support for working with the erotic. She also, in the current climate, was afraid of getting it wrong if she were to engage in working with a client's erotic feelings (or indeed her own) or of the client taking it the wrong way.

My colleague, Leanne O'Shea has written elsewhere of the danger that the restating of an ethical principle does nothing to manage the actuality of sexual attraction between client and therapist. Rules on their own do absolutely nothing to holistically manage the kinds of feelings that are bound to emerge between two people in an environment that is often intense and intimate (O'Shea, 2000). She takes the view that the client's sexuality will *always* be present in the therapeutic encounter.

I recall one of my male clients with whom I would often feel a deep and exquisite pleasure in his company that felt sexualised. Even though on a conscious level I was not physically attracted to him, my body felt alive when I was around him and in anticipation of his arrival. What this "information" helped me to know was how much this man, who as a baby was left with his mother for several years while his father was fighting in the war, needed to make his mother–who was no doubt lonely, worried and frightened–feel good. Being open to my erotic countertransference helped me to bring into the in-between my knowledge of how hard he had worked as a little boy and continued to work as a man to become perfectly attuned to women who never found him quite perfect enough. His gradual awareness of this helped us to begin to explore what it would be like for him to care for and take delight and pleasure in himself.

(SS) Through talking with colleagues and supervisees I have come to appreciate how the issues of sex, sexuality and the erotic are so often the cause of awkwardness and embarrassment that can feel almost like trespassing on "sacred ground." This would seem to suggest that issues of sexuality and sex are highly sensitive areas for exploration because they go to the core of an individual's personal and unique sense of self. As well as this sensitivity for the "sacred" there are also fears of the erotic as a destructive force to be avoided or defended against at all costs.

Whereas erotic transference and countertransference may be shied away from, it would appear that negative transferential emotions such as anger and hate are proactively dodged! Listening to colleagues and supervisees it is my belief that we all struggle and are uneasy, even afraid, of love and hate as they reveal themselves in the twists and turns of the therapeutic journey. Indeed, perhaps for some of us the expression of powerful emotion is such a dangerous taboo that we desensitise (push out of awareness or repress) our loving and hateful experiences of ourselves and our clients. In this way our therapeutic receptivity to love and hate is impaired. Particularly, I wonder, how do we as therapists know when a client's powerful "negative" feelings towards us–rage, anger, fear, stubbornness, rebellion–become impossible for the client to express because of their unconscious knowledge that we won't be able to take it? And how do we as therapists use these feelings when they well up in us?

(AK) I worked for many years with a woman who I found it hard to see in any other way than utterly miserable. Every area of her life was bleak. She had no hope that things could be different. I often felt useless and despairing and, although I was encouraged to empathise with how useless *she* must have felt, no amount of supervision could help me to reach her. One day she came and announced that she had been thinking about how easy it would be to kill herself when she was driving the long distances on motorways that her job required. This in itself was a sort of progress as if was the first time that she talked about thinking in any way that she could take any action at all to change her circumstances. I took her suicidal thoughts seriously and strongly suggested to her that she come for an extra appointment at the end of the week or, at least, that she ring me. When I didn't hear from her I was surprised at my reaction. I didn't feel concerned. I felt angry. In fact, my internal response to the question, "I wonder if she *has* killed herself", was a loud and emphatic "Good"! I shocked myself but stayed with the thoughts and feelings until I realized that I would only have such an intense reaction towards someone that I loved who would not accept that love. By allowing an apparently hateful reaction to inform the work I arrived at a place of softness and vulnerability that allowed me to be with my client, who came to her next appointment feeling rather chirpy, in a different, more tolerant and connected way.

Re-claiming the erotic: turning to love

Through this discourse we want to re-claim the erotic in the therapeutic journey. We are offering an understanding of the client's erotic deficits, traumas and conflicts as they become figural in the relationship. We are also offering some guidance on how to identify and work with our clients' erotic transference and out own erotic countertransference. We want to utilise the erotic dialogue—the unique emotional interpenetration between client and therapist—as a way of understanding and addressing our client's developmental derailments or deficits.

We do not align ourselves, however, with the classical psychoanalytic position that the erotic is the *sine qua non* of psychotherapy. Within the frame of classical psychoanalysis erotic transference is understood as resistance—as a way of seducing the therapist from entering the patient's deeper, intra-psychic world—that needs to be dissolved; and/or comprehended as a memory of incestuous oedipal love for a parent which is being projected onto the analyst. This, it is argued, needs to be resolved by gentle frustration until the patient turns his or her erotic desires outwards to a more appropriate external love object. Clearly, sometimes the erotic can manifest itself as a way of distracting the therapist from entering the client's deeper world. However, we concur with Mann (1997) who maintains that if the erotic is therapeutically worked with it can transform the patient's psyche at a deep level and help modify aggressive and hateful feelings.

More explicitly Mann (1997, p. 8) maintains that:

"This transformational quality of the erotic is at the heart of love. When in love, the lover is seeking the most intimate experience one can find with another. Lovers wish to know the details of the other's emotional life: they exchange secrets, share night-time and day-time dreams; They probe each other physically and psychologically to explore their own depth and the depth of the other. In this way they reach new heights and new lows. When in love, people wish to be completely known and understood by the beloved. They wish to transform themselves into somebody even more loveable, to improve their faults and change bad habits or anything dislikeable about themselves."

Therefore, the emergence of the client's love in the transference holds the potential for transformation through relational engagement between therapist and client. The therapist's capacity for managing erotic countertransference is essential in meeting the client's erotic deficits, traumas and conflicts. In effect the therapist's personal readiness and professional robustness to work with the erotic in covert and overt ways signals to the client—consciously and unconsciously—that their hope is not misplaced: that the therapist is willing to emotionally and psychologically be penetrated by the client's erotic triumphs, catastrophes and disappointments. In this way we can resonate with Bollas' (1987) concept of the (m)other as the transformational object, which is then transposed on to the role of the therapist. As a transformational object the therapist holds and contains the client's archaic erotic and hateful feelings. Furthermore, the therapist responds in an accepting and non-shaming way, and this relational receptivity helps to mediate and modulate these highly charged transferences. Working with the client's unconscious and conscious love and hate steers the relationship to work through unaddressed developmental deficits, traumas and conflicts in respect of love and hate. Finally, to maximize this potential for transformation, the therapist needs to monitor his counter-transferential material and avoid defensive responses such as withdrawal, sexually acting-out or shaming, and/or attacking the client, so often reminiscent of the client's early history.

Mann believes that the erotic "is the very creative stuff of life and is inextricably linked to passion". He sees in the erotic its "ability" to elicit the unexpected as the therapeutic momentum. Love or the erotic cannot be defined he says, as it is not possible to take a detached stance from such basic human qualities. There is, he says, "only passion, sometimes hot or cold or all the degrees in between (1997, p. 5)". He goes on to say that he sees love as a mixture of past and future as they converge in the present: the regressive element in love impels us to seek and rediscover something from the past. In this sense, love is an attempt to restore a lost unity. It is this regressive pull of love that is in the foreground of an erotic transference (p. 8). Repetition can be seen as an attempt to heal past disappointments–to transform the individual into something better, stronger, healthier, more alive, more complete, more mature and more developed. Through the psyche the erotic seeks growth. It provides the mechanism and the impetus to transform our unconscious life.

Having said this Mann reminds us that transference love is real love. "Far from being a problem to be avoided it may be considered a development the patient and therapist have been lucky enough to encounter, and though not to be encouraged, at least considered benign once it is manifest" (p. 23). Mann therefore believes that most love is provoked by the situation and that certain kinds of relationship are likely to foster certain aspects of loving. Where there are power imbalances–such as in the psychotherapeutic setting–there will be a greater emphasis on parent/child love. Such love, however, is not a repetition, but contains a desire for a new transformational object. So, we believe, does any kind of love. Also, as Mann says *any* kind of love is intensified when the object of affection is coy or "plays hard to get".

It's probably fair to say that most clients come into therapy because, at some level, they are experiencing problems in their loving relationships. In these cases the partner is usually too similar in some aspects to one or both parents. This is the repetition compulsion or the fixed gestalt at work. Our partners need to fall within our relational orbit. The goal of therapy then could be described as expanding the client's relational range.

Having begun the essential journey of re-claiming the erotic in the co-created space between client and therapist we would now like to deepen this understanding by exploring the developmental roots and language of the erotic.

The pre-oedipal "Love affair" between baby and mother

Many object relations writers (Klein, 1945; Winnicott, 1965; Balint, 1968 etc.) have attempted to capture the essence of the dynamic interplay or emotional "dance" between baby and mother through the formative years (0–3/4 years of age) known as the pre-verbal or pre-oedipal phase. Gomez (1997) outlines the primary relational focus of the different phases seeing issues of trust, dependency and power over others as belonging to the pre-verbal phases and issues of sexuality, status and competition as emerging in the Oedipal phase. Object relations is not a unified corpus of work but a disparate body of theory that has been added to by different clinicians. However, collectively, object relations theorists highlight the primacy of relationships and uphold the belief that human beings are essentially relationship-seeking. In effect object relations writers have attempted to move beyond Freud's drive theory, which understands human strivings as motivated by almost animal instincts that must be controlled or at least tamed (Freud, 1930/2001). In essence a more unitary view of human beings has been attempted by bringing together the biological need for food, drink, shelter and sex with the psychological need for relationship, intimacy and meaning-making.

In more recent years, Stern (2004) has deepened our knowledge of the baby's innate drive towards relationship. He believes that the "erotic love affair" between baby and mother begins very early on. Through his pioneering research, he claims that the physical language of love has been performed, repeated and learned by the fourth and fifth months of life. For example, Stern identifies the non-verbal contact and physical expression that take place between baby and mother: their faces are often inches apart; facial communication is exaggerated and reciprocated; parts of their bodies are often touching; there are gestures of kissing, hugging, touching and holding each others faces and hands. In terms of physical contact both baby and mother simultaneously move from an approach-approach to withdraw-withdraw contact which is repeated time and again in tune with each other's emotional and psychological needs. This reciprocal and rhythmical "dance" is a typical hallmark of newly found lovers. He further notes that it is only intimates such as lovers and babies who transcend the cultural norms that govern and modulate personal space and proximity in social settings.

As well as the non-verbal communications between baby and mother Stern also highlights the musical register of speech between the two over and above the lyrics being employed and how this resonates with lovers caught-up in communication with each other. It is as if the symphonic melody between baby and mother transmits and communicates the love, pleasure and enjoyment of being (almost) singularly preoccupied with the other; again this is characteristic of newly fledged lovers. Stern also studied the intense mutual gaze that is exchanged between baby and mother at two and a half months that can last for tens of seconds or even minutes. This mutually charged gaze without speaking is rarely repeated with such intensity in everyday adult life. Indeed, he says that "If two adults look into each others eyes without talking for more than five seconds or so, they are likely to fight or make love" (p. 177). We would add or be therapist and client! Given the non-verbal expressions, the carefully negotiated closeness and separation, and the eye contact that occurs between client and therapist it is hardly surprising that client and therapist "fall in love" and/or want to fight!

Throughout this critical early stage (0–5 months old) and beyond, up to the beginning of the Oedipal phase (3/4 years of age), the baby has registered the procedural knowledge and sensory-motor schemas that are "imprinted" in the motor memories. In other words the physical and emotional language of "erotic love" has become the prototype from which the developing child, teenager and adult will express his desires, longings and love in his future erotic life. But what happens if this vital experience between baby and mother is impaired or derailed? If these essential early erotic excitations are lacking or transgressed what will happen to the emerging adult's erotic sensuality? What is needed therapeutically to address these deficits and derailments?

(SS): Barry

Barry is a 33-year-old white British male who came to therapy with relationship problems. He worked in the music business as a manager of would be music artists and bands. He was unable to maintain sustaining and erotically pleasing relationships with woman. He would "fall head over heels" but within weeks would be disenchanted and terminate the relationship. He was an attractive, muscular and well presented man. As the therapeutic relationship emerged it became clear that he had construed a schizoid defence to avoid emotional engagement and keep safely within his head through intellectualisation. This made sense given his early hostile family history: his father had been highly critical, ridiculing and attacking of his son from Barry's earliest memories. If he upset his father he would be punished. Sometimes Barry's father would ignore him for weeks, even months. His mother would feel compromised and align herself with Barry's father. Barry has one sibling, a sister, who suffers from paranoid schizophrenia.

In the early stages of therapy we explored his brief highly romantic relationships with women and his platonic relationships with men. His "failure" with women is listed above and his relational contact with men was absent. At one point when exploring how he felt working with a male therapist he declared: "I don't see you as a man and I don't see you as a woman either. You're just Steven". This de-sexualisation of an important other was a common theme that we would return to again and again: clearly, the erotic excitations between mother and baby were severely impaired. I began to see his successive courtships and abrupt endings with women as an unconscious expression of un-addressed rage towards his mother. Furthermore, I wondered whether his experience of his father made him wary of male friends. As I explored these possibilities sensitively and tentatively with Barry he began to allow me to penetrate his defended world in order for him to share his grief, anger and deep disappointment about his parents' lack of pleasure in and enjoyment of him. Likewise he wanted to know whether he was impacting me in someway.

It was during this phase that Barry would frequently touch his groin area and with legs widely apart make slight thrusting motions with his pelvis and groin. It was clear that this not in his conscious awareness. I was aware that I initially felt uncomfortable, sexually aroused and confused. Gradually I realised that Barry was looking for erotic approval, enjoyment and pleasure from a significant other in order to feel desirable and loveable. I was challenged to find personal resources to enjoy this man–emotionally, psychologically and aesthetically enjoy his looks, physique and character–in order to address his earliest deficits and traumas in the therapeutic dialogue.

A great deal of the erotic excitation that I felt and Barry longed for was unspoken but held and communicated in non-verbal and unconscious ways. I learnt this lesson from a misguided intervention. Barry was sharing with me that he had been away for a weekend to manage the next "would-be" boy band. One evening after the gig he was sleeping while the band members got drunk and began being rowdy downstairs. He went down to stop them and encourage them to go to bed.

> *Barry:* "So I jumped out of bed and put my baggy boxer shorts on and went down to confront them and I was really assertive!"
>
> *Steven:* "How did they respond to you?"
>
> *Barry:* "They apologised and stopped and then one of them said "Hey Barry! Look at the size of you!" (*Barry giggles and looks embarrassed*) And then after that for the whole week they called me Moby!"
>
> *Steven:* "Moby?" (*feeling aroused*)
>
> *Barry:* "As in the whale!" (*A double entendre playing on the name of Herman Melville classic book Moby-Dick*)
>
> *Steven:* "You mean dick, like penis or cock?"

Barry: "Oh! You said a naughty word then". (*he blushes and drops his head*).

To my surprise, despite the seemingly adult nature of the conversation between the Band and Barry, and Barry and me I had overlooked the fact that my arousal was information that he was in a regressed state. I redeemed this potentially difficult moment by focusing on how he felt that they had noticed that he more than measured-up and that they were admiring of him. This course of action re-engaged Barry in the secure and intimate nature of our attachment and he was able to experience the pre-occupation of an erotically affirming other that had been so lacking in his early development.

A general rule of thumb is that if erotic feelings are experienced by the therapist in the countertransference and are not verbalised by the client, then chances are that this erotic material is coming from a pre-verbal place. It is vital, therefore, that the therapists sexual interest, pleasure and enjoyment—so missing from the client's early developmental years–is kept at this non-verbal level and not named overtly. In other words if a client names that they find you attractive, pretty or handsome then we are probably dealing with the oedipal or verbal level of erotic transference and this needs to be met and worked through at the verbal level. We will return to this below.

Much later towards the end of three years of therapy Barry was able to talk about his masculinity and sexuality in an adult way and he began to choose partners that honoured the romantic and erotic "triumphs" and "failures" of his sexual love life. My erotic investment and enjoyment of him empowered Barry to get his derailed erotic desires, longings and expressions back on track in a creative, enjoyable and transformative way.

(AK): I recall talking with a colleague about a male client with a schizoid self-process who desperately longed to be physically held as a visceral way of making contact and yet, as is typical of a client with a schizoid presentation, was terrified of being touched. He longed for skin-to-skin contact as a way of connecting with the world he had for so long defended against through rationalisation and intellectualisation. In accordance with the client's story his

mother was generally unable to take pleasure and enjoyment in him and we postulated that this key form of communication was probably sadly missing through his pre-oedipal formative years. What was really important for my colleague was to hold to therapeutic and ethical boundaries and not offer physical touch. In a session the client named how he longed to touch the therapist. In that moment she replied: "Ah! but you do touch me!" The client was deeply moved by this interchange. It is these moments–touching the client with carefully monitored and mediated words and affect—that can provide opportunities of developmental repair and transformation.

Questioning the oedipal love song of "Conquer and divide"

Returning to the issue of overtly working with erotic transference let us also return to the Oedipal triangle as postulated by Freud (1930/2001). He saw *eros* (the life instinct) and *thanatos* (the death instinct) as unconscious, conflicting drives creating psychic tension. Furthermore, he believed that the psyche was ruled by the "pleasure principle" with its pursuit of gratifying amoral, instinctual needs and its avoidance of pain. The triangular relationship of the Oedipus Complex (3/4 years of age) is perhaps one of the most well known examples of how the child has to work through conflicting feelings of love and hate towards his parents as it dawns upon him that his mother is not exclusively his, but "shared" with his father. Likewise, this process for girls is labelled by Freud as the Electra complex: the desire of the female child to "overthrow and banish her mother" and claim the father for herself. The child has to wrestle with his unconscious (primary) process and its impulsive drive towards pleasure: his sexual wish to "conquer" his mother and his aggressive desire to compete with and banish his father. With any luck his parents understand this dilemma and with love firmly abstain from gratifying these instinctual needs. This strengthens his conscious (secondary) processes and his sense of reality (the "reality principle"), which enables him to manage his frustration, anger and rage as he encounters delayed, and non-gratification in the wider world (Freud, 1900/2001).

In Freud's view the Oedipal triangle (mother, father and baby) is seen as potentially incestuous and regarded as a developmental crisis in respect of the child's emerging sexual orientation. There is an understanding that the positive and negative bisexual oedipal constellations–it is acknowledged that the child will oscillate between his wish to conquer and possess one parent and banish the other with both the opposite sex gender parent and the same sex gender parent–have to be overcome in favour of heterosexual primacy. An Oedipal "victory" (excluding one parent and triumphing over them by aligning with the remaining parent's exclusive attention and adoration) with the opposite-sex parent or the same-sex parent is regarded as dangerous, with the latter being labelled pathological. Consequently, the classical psychoanalytic treatment to remedy this is to interpret the patient's erotic desires, longings and yearnings by holding a non-participatory and non-gratifying analytical stance. This will increase the patient's erotic charge and therefore, erotic longing for the analyst. In turn the analyst is expected to use interpretation to make the unconscious conscious (name the oedipal replay) and thereby empower the patient to transcend the primary impulses with choice, autonomy and self-direction. In other words dissolve the power of the "psychical hold" of the incestuous Oedipal triangle and direct the patient outwards to external objects (appropriate lovers) outside of the psychoanalytic container.

We take exception to a number of held beliefs surrounding classical psychoanalysis' understanding of the Oedipal phase of development. Firstly, we do not believe that heterosexuality is the only normal outcome of the Oedipal phase, and secondly we do not believe that Oedipal conflicts are somehow resolved once and for all, either in the Oedipal triangle itself or in later adult analysis. Messler-Davies (2003) offers a powerful critique of the traditional psychoanalytic treatment of oedipal material arguing that by the analyst being unavailable, discounting the sexual transference and by being non-relational (non-gratifying and non-participatory) the patient becomes locked in "erotic masochism". Hence, the patient becomes locked in the oedipal triangular transference and becomes ensnared in a destructive and frustrating cycle of unrequited love: romantically pursuing idealised, "perfect" and therefore unavailable lovers. In our view erotically defeated adults emerge from these processes that try to deny the real presence of the therapist. However, Steven recalls a moment of extreme discomfort when a client overtly named towards erotically charged transferences towards him.

(SS) Lily

Lily is a 27-year-old mixed race woman (mother is white British and father is Afro-Caribbean who she describes as handsome) who is single. She is extremely beautiful and works as a model. Her earliest memory of her mother was that she suffered from psychosis and was frequently sectioned under the Mental Health Act. Lily was in and out of children's homes from 6 years onwards where she recalls frequent sexual abuse. Her father left the family home when she was three years old. What became clear was that Lily qualified for a DSM IV borderline personality diagnosis. In the first meeting Lily followed me into the therapy room and I asked her to take a seat. As she sat down she declared:

> Lily: (aggressively) "You do know that I don't want to see a man! I'd prefer to see a woman, but the waiting list is too long!"
>
> Steven: (feeling on alert) "Yes I have been told that. And I can also see that you are of mixed race and I am white and I wonder how you feel about that too?"
>
> Lily: (calmly) "Well I am so confused ... when I am with black people, I don't feel black enough and when I'm with white people, I don't feel white enough. I don't know whether I am straight or gay or bisexual. I just don't know where I belong".

What emerged over many months was Lily's fragile sense of self and her psychological confusion: she would often say that she did not feel black enough to be black or white enough to be white. Furthermore, she did not know whether she was heterosexual, homosexual or bisexual. As well as her constant pursuit of very attractive, male high achiever's who were unavailable to her, Lily would frequently wear provocative clothes to our sessions and say outrageous sexual comments to shock me. Initially, I understood that this was part of her borderline process to determine whether I too would reject or abandon her like her parents. However, as I tuned in to the erotic transference I began to realise that she was attempting to evoke sexual interest, intrigue and admiration from me. At first I remember pulling away and not being able to tolerate her erotic advances. Eventually I realised that the more I did this the more Lily would relentlessly pursue me. I was scared that any resonance or affirmation of her sexual beauty would invite unwanted sexual overtures from Lily and I did not want to place my client or myself in a non-professional and unethical compromise. However, the more I pulled away the more she pursued me!

Through supervision I was able to recognise my client's longing to be erotically enjoyed and gained compassion for her severe lack of a baby–(m)other love affair and the unavailability of her "handsome" but distant father. Gradually I learned to risk small pieces of judicious self-disclosure of my erotic countertransference only when it was directly solicited or invited. To do otherwise would have over-stimulated, frightened and/or confused Lily and put me at risk.

The therapeutic relationship became more intimate and emotionally inter-penetrating within a reciprocal mutuality. One day she brought some photograph albums of her modelling work and was keen to hear how I viewed her: "Gosh!", I said, "You look stunning!" Eventually Lily asked outright whether I found her attractive or not:

Lily: "Do you think I am attractive?"

Steven: "Yes! I do. (allowing time for her to take this in) I imagine most people do (allowing a bit more time) and I also would never cross your personal boundaries like what happened to you in the children's homes"

Lily: "Thank you" (softly spoken, as she cried)

In time after being erotically receptive and expressive with Lily it became apparent that it was time to gradually allow, what Messler-Davis (2003) terms, a relinquishing of the erotically held idealisation of self and other. Eventually, through dialoguing we were able to allow the transference to dissolve and honour that we were not erotically ideal–each of us where flawed; a mixture of good and bad, light and shadow: imperfection was tolerated, accepted and understood as healthy! This led Lily to explore that she didn't have to be erotically perfect to be lovable–likewise, I was not the erotically ideal father she longed for. This process led us to evaluate other interpersonal attributes—such as kindness, assertiveness, self-care, anger, honesty–and how these made someone as equally as attractive as their looks. Lily was able to step-out and discover external love choices who where available, less idealised and more real. Through this phase of the journey we were able to celebrate romantic triumphs and mourn and accept romantic defeats. In this way Lily was able to experience love and hate, and to be both winner and loser in the game of love. Her sexual attachments were now being coloured by these experiences in a way that deepened her erotic creativity and prepared her for real loving relationships.

We want emphatically to say that to risk erotic self-disclosure when it has not been elicited or asked for should be avoided at all costs. Doing so may be experienced by the client as the therapist being seductive and/or manipulative and will blur the boundaries of the therapeutic frame putting both client and therapist at risk. The same goes for inappropriate sexual remarks or innuendo. We've just heard a story of a male therapist who, listening to a lonely but attractive woman describe how her Buddhist spiritual practice was a great support to her, replied, "But that won't get you a shag, will it?" The therapist was lucky. The client had enough internal support to be satisfied with writing informally to the therapist and his professional organisation to express her discomfort. She did not take out a formal complaint though she easily could have done. And won!

This sort of victory, though, particularly when it comes after a lengthy therapeutic relationship is a kind of Oedipal victory involving a killing off or exiling of the therapist (parent) that will not be enriching to the client's relational life.

As we reflect on the examples above we are keen to explore the shadow side of the erotic. What happens when our countertransference, far from informing us of erotic pleasure, enjoyment and delight in our client, stirs us up with disgust or even repulsion?

Erotic countertransference: repulsion

(AK): Tomkins (1962) posits nine innate affects, two of which are *disgust* and *dissmell*. If disgust is a word indicating a bad taste, dissmell, Tomkins says, is our innate reaction to a bad smell. The facial characteristics are upper lip wrinkled and head pulled back. The body may also withdraw distancing itself from the source of the bad smell. Dissmell is our early warning system for toxic or harmful substances. Dissmell and disgust may operate independently or together at different intensities. Anyone on the receiving end of the dissmell affect, being treated as if they smell bad, will suffer reduced self-esteem and thus experience shame (Nathanson, 1992, p. 125).

Dissmell and disgust, then, start out as hard-wired responses to smells and tastes outside an infant's acceptable sensory range. As the infant matures in relationship with others she encounters situations in which how someone is or what someone does falls outside an acceptable range. In that sense, such people or actions may trigger the responses to which we grew accustomed as small children—dissmell for people we wish to keep at a distance, and disgust for people with whom we have been intimately involved and from which we would like to get away. The physiological mechanisms that evolved for bad smell and taste come to operate as mental representations for actions and people, even people who in no way actually trigger nasal or oral reactions.

I remember Rena, a male to female transsexual, who told me about running into an old school friend. She greeted him, saying, "You look exactly the same!" The friend looked at Rena quizzically and said, "Not you mate! Are you going to a fancy dress or something?" She was crushed but hid her feelings behind a rather acerbic mask, telling the story as though it was amusing. And I winced. As much as I felt warmth and admiration for Rena who was a few years away from having final gender reassignment surgery she looked ridiculous. She would have *known* this from my automatic reaction to seeing her when I opened the door for the first session. I took Rena's risking telling me how she felt about how her friend reacted to be a message in code that she knew what she could not yet own: that she did not look like a "real" woman and probably never would. In struggling to find a place where I could identify with Rena and not wanting to shame her with a directly empathic response that might have rubbed salt into an already open wound I found an aspect of my own experience that I decided to share with her.

Anne: "It's so hard to be seen by others in a way that's different to how you see yourself".

Rena: (looking interested and not in touch with her pain)

> *Anne:* "You know after twenty-something years of living in England and no longer *feeling* American I sometimes feel crushed when people seem to have to remind me that I *sound* American no matter how I feel".

This intervention and moment of connection between us had the effect of supporting Rena to bring to the therapy her knowledge that she would never be a biological woman no matter how much she protested that she *was* a woman.

Re-claiming thanatos: turning to hate

Winnicott's seminal work *"Hate in the Countertransference"* (1947, p. 199) provides us with a theoretical and clinical frame of reference to more fully understand this primary emotion as it reveals itself in the in-between of therapy. As you read this you may be aware of feeling resistant or uncomfortable at the invitation to acknowledge, face and explore transferential and counter-transferential hateful feelings. We appreciate this and we hope to empower practitioners to overcome their possible denial or projection of this particular emotion and begin to appreciate the enormous therapeutic potential working with hate might provide. Furthermore, we hope to highlight the potentially harmful or even destructive counter-therapeutic outcome if hate is ignored or "banished" (if such a thing were possible) from the therapeutic encounter.

When speaking of the child's developmental needs, Winnicott (1947, p. 199) boldly claimed that: "What happens is that after a while a child (here of a broken home or without parents) gains hope, and then he starts to test out the environment he has found, and to seek proof of the guardians' ability to hate object-ively. It seems that he can believe in being loved only after reaching being hated".

In essence this developmental understanding is transferred to the therapeutic dyad between the "analytic-child" and "analytic-parent". Our understanding is that when our clients are repetitive, resistant to care or change, aggressive, ungrateful, demanding or disgusting we will be provoked to feel hateful counter-transferential feelings. By the same token our clients will exhibit transferential hate towards us: in the transferential vacillations we are often perceived in idealised terms—we don't have any problems or have painful or difficult days! The envy and resentment towards our "perfected state of being" will inevitably invite intense feelings of hate. So what do we do?

Winnicott gives us "permission" to face what, in the humanistic tradition, might be otherwise unacceptable negative reactions as they emerge in the therapeutic relationship. This permission affords us the freedom to talk about transferential and counter-transferential hate with colleagues, in supervision and in our personal therapy taking hate out of the shadow where it has been lurking all along. We hope that this freedom helps us to develop a greater capacity to tolerate hateful clinical material without *doing* anything about it. Ironically, we believe that when hateful feelings are not acknowledged and clinically owned and worked with, there is a higher risk of destructive acting-out between client and therapist. Gabbard (2003) maintains that the analyst's rage and despair (hate) may be in direct response to the patient's failure to get better, thus diminishing the analyst's omnipotent strivings to heal. He recalls a story by Celenza (1991) who describes a therapist who could not tolerate his client's negative transference and his own negative countertransference feelings. The therapy was at an impasse. Unable to tolerate the discomfort and to see it as a necessary part of the therapy, the therapist embarked on a sexual relationship with his client as an unconscious attempt to bypass all the negative feelings and to foster instead a more comfortable idealising transference.

In line with Winnicott's belief that hate needs to be acknowledged by the mother so that the child can feel "real" we would contend that our clients unconsciously (out of awareness) need us to recognise *our* hate so they can feel real. There is a kind of parallel here with the notion that our "YES" will have no emotional meaning or depth until we have learnt to say "NO!".

You may have noticed Winnicott's specific emphasis for the therapist to have the *"ability to hate object-ively"*. This is in sharp contradistinction to hating *subject-ively* which means the therapist's personal hate as it surfaces from her beliefs, values and prejudices. This material—hate towards a client for their accent or envious hate towards the client for being out of work and paying an agreed reduced fee–belongs to the therapist individually and to society collectively and therefore needs to be processed through self-reflection and supervision. Hence, the ability to hate *object-ively* refers to the therapist's ability to respond to the client's unfinished business in respect of developmental traumas, deficits and conflicts as they are re-played in the space in-between. These are the feelings of hate that are likely to arise in response, say, to the client's persistent testing of boundaries or the client's "ungrateful" refusal to acknowledge change. This does not mean that the therapist is free to engage in promiscuous self-disclosure of his less-than-savoury feelings. Rather, "... hate that is justified in the present setting has to be sorted out and kept in storage and available for eventual interpretation" (Winnicott, 1947, p. 196). It is the role of the therapist to hold these hateful counter-transferences (possibly even until the ending stage of the therapeutic journey) and translate them into therapeutic interventions and responses that empower the client to feel real, rounded and whole. Let's consider the example of the persistent pushing of professional and personal boundaries by the client. Once this testing stage has passed and the client begins to use the therapeutic space to deepen his knowledge of himself there may be occasion to feed back this particular counter-transferential hate so that it can be re-owned (re-introjected). For example the therapist might say something like: "As you share with me that you realise how you push people around, I am aware that I often felt irritated and pushed around too in the early stages of our work together".

This reveals a real meeting in the in-between and communicates that the therapist was able to bear the client's negative feelings without emotionally withdrawing or retaliating. But what happens when this opportunity does not transpire?

(SS): Peter

Peter is a 25-year-old white British man who was referred to a counselling service by the local secondary care MH hospital. (At the time of referral I was 12 years older than my client.) Peter had been given a diagnosis of Narcissistic Personality Disorder and wanted to explore his grief at losing his male partner of three years standing who had died two years previously, and his childhood history. At the time of his partner's death (who was aged 67) Peter dramatically de-compensated and became psychotic, unable to relate to others and to cope with reality. He was sectioned under the Mental Health Act at this time and twelve months later was supported by the

Community Mental Health Team to re-habilitate and begin to take up work and eventually occupy his own flat. At the time when we began to work together Peter had been living in a flat of his own for six months. He had been holding down a gardening job four days a week, which he thoroughly enjoyed.

In the first couple of months that we worked together Peter revealed how he had been constantly and verbally punished by his mother, who was a born–again Christian, for being a bad, naughty and dirty child. His father, who was a merchant seaman, was regularly absent for several months at a time. When his father was at home with the family he would invariably sit behind a newspaper. From the age of five onwards Peter would climb the attic steps and hide in the hope someone would come and find him. This, he recalls, never happened and he would have to return to the living room to a wall of distraction and silence.

In the countertransference I felt like Peter wanted to drive me away, to abandon him or even reject him. During this time Peter asked me whether I found him attractive, which I did not. It took careful and sensitive negotiation to share this in a non-rejecting or non-shaming way. He was able to bear this because we concluded that lots of people would and do find him attractive. In contrast to this, when accessing his grief for his partner he would begin to disconnect and withdraw into a psychotic transference, hiding in his "psychological attic". This flight from reality and complexity was, in my mind, Peter's need to regress to a psychotic, objectless state as a way of avoiding pain and even terror. Through supervision we agreed that it was important not to pursue Peter when he regressed like this but to gently call him back into the reality of the moment.

The middle phase of our work was the most disturbing and challenging time. One day Peter revealed that as he sat with me he was wearing a disposable adult nappy into which he had urinated and defecated and that he found this sexually exciting. He told me how he would find older men via the internet who would come to his home and clean him-up after he had messed his nappy—wash him and powder him and then have sex with him. Through supervision I was able to own my disgust and my impulsive reaction to pull away. I found it very difficult to find empathy or understanding for Peter. In fact I found him disgusting. Again my supervisor and I postulated that he wanted me to abandon him and not find any pleasure and enjoyment in him, which was so resonant with his childhood environment. My supervisor helped me to understand the comfort a baby who felt all alone might feel feeling warm urine against his body. This also helped me to access a memory of how I, as a little child of six attending primary school, had a mishap and soiled my trousers and felt great shame. In time I was able to find compassion for Peter whose only way of dealing with his developmental trauma was to return to a state of primary narcissism–a form of self-love so characteristic of infants. This regression became sexualised for my client–a travesty of the healthy erotic emotional and psychological enjoyment he so longed for.

I came to realise that this regression—while the most creative Peter could arrive at in order to cope with his narcissistic injuries–was what Balint (1968) called a "malignant regression". Balint captured the essence of creative and destructive aspects of human motivation with his notion of "benign" and "malignant regressions". The former refers to the client regressing *with* the therapist in a reciprocal, inter-subjective meeting in order to mend his sense of being broken. The latter signifies a destructive process in which the client seemingly searches for emotional contact but is afraid of the consequences. Out of fear he looks to the power of the therapist, not for relationship, but for a gratifying merging as a way of avoiding painful psychic memories of early loss.

In the final stage of the work Peter revealed—after I enquired noticing a severe increase in his psychotic transference–that he was taking copious amounts of cocaine. At this point I asked him not to take drugs twelve hours before our session because this would interfere with our work. The policy of the counselling agency also requested this. At this point Peter exploded into narcissistic rage and attempted to leave the room. I managed to persuade him to stay and tell me how he felt rather than leave in a heightened state of anger. As Peter shouted aggressively during the remaining thirty minutes I realised that he had now found a way to make me the parent he so longed to hate and destroy. He did return the following week and announced he was leaving to join Buddhist meditation classes that clashed with his therapy day and time slot. I offered some of my thoughts to Peter who shouted, "You should not respond to me; you should just sit there and listen and say nothing!" Ultimately I was not able to support Peter to stay and work through his rage. We had worked together for six months.

Gomez (1997) writes that clients with Oedipal phase issues may cast the therapist in the role of the powerful, desirable, glamorous parent or, conversely, as dowdy, embarrassing or repulsive. She reminds us that the therapist may also become the frightening judge condemning the client's forbidden wishes or the killjoy pouring cold water on his excitement (p. 186). This, I believe, is what happened with Peter when I confronted his drug use, calling upon the agency's guidelines to contain *my* discomfort in a way that did not help Peter to contain his rage.

Love

Storr (1999) has written: "in the practice of his art, the therapist must treat those patients who make declarations of love with tenderness and understanding. It is important to realise that the love which is shown by the patient for the therapist is just as "genuine", even though it may not be as realistic, as love occurring outside the therapeutic situation" (p. 8). This is especially important with clients who believe their love is bad or toxic.

(AK) I have written earlier (Kearns, 2005) about my work with a schizoid client called Nigel who was fearful that if he admitted to sexual or loving feelings I might punish him for feeling good. He came to "intellectually" consider that I cared for him but said it was too risky for him to allow himself to *feel* my care. We were able to talk about his fear that I might be repelled by his love and could reject him. The truth is that I felt the most exquisite tenderness for Nigel and cherished every expression of liveliness that he was brave enough to show me, like a new mother with baby's first smile. Most of these expressions were out of his awareness and I was careful not to spoil them by calling them to his attention. I showed him how I felt for him and how I instinctively responded to him through my facial expressions which, after ten years of working together, many of which were spent looking "through" me, he became increasingly able to receive and to return.

I want to add a postscript to that example. In a recent session Nigel was able to talk about his need to have a woman in his life that loved him. He looked at me and said, "But you love me, don't you". I haven't put a question mark at the end of that phrase as it felt to me more a statement than a question. I replied, "You seem to know that I do". For Nigel that was enough.

Yalom (1980) reminds us that a client's questions about love may be part of a struggle for control in the relationship. This was not the case with Nigel, as I didn't feel the "squirm-factor" that Yalom describes. Yet I did not answer Nigel's question directly. Writing in the person centred tradition Tudor and Worrall (2006) remind us that the "task of psychotherapy is to make thoughts clear and to give them sharp boundaries" (p. 15). How ever tempting it is for the therapist to respond truthfully and instinctively with declarations of love–or of any other powerful emotion–we need to heed Yalom's reminder that what makes the therapeutic relationship different from a loving friendship is that it lacks reciprocity. As a therapist I have to hold in my mind that, however much I may come to love my clients, it is also part of my job to work from the start in the full knowledge that goal of this relationship is for it to come to an end.

Conclusion

We have attempted here to provide a theoretical framework that champions transferential and countertransferential love and hate in the "in-between". This has not been an exhaustive work but rather our collective effort to enable humanistic practitioners to begin to enjoy the conceptual and practical freedom to honour these emotive expressions as they appear in the co-created space between client and therapist. We hope that the clinical examples cited above have also drawn out some tangible guidelines when it comes to clinical practice and will give you permission to explore love and hate with colleagues, supervisors and in your own therapy.

CHAPTER FIVE

Working through an impasse

Patti Owens

C athy came into therapy because she wanted to understand what she saw as a self-destructive need to "act a role" rather than really being herself. She had also been taking antidepressants at intervals over the last twenty years. Although on the surface happily married, she was concerned that people easily got bored with her and relationships often faltered or ended prematurely. She had been in therapy before but stopped just as she was on the threshold of doing "deeper" work.

We worked together for nearly a year and my four-week summer holiday was two weeks away. I had made a mental note that Cathy was likely to defend against her anxieties about such a long break by filling the session with anecdotal and distancing material and that I would need to help her to focus on her feelings about the upcoming break. In the penultimate session I neglected to do this, letting Cathy tell me stories about a difficulty she was having with someone else. I came to the last session before the break with a firm resolve to do better next time. Somehow I again failed to do this, only briefly touching on the implications of the break and struggling with feeling uncharacteristically sleepy and bored.

Rupture

Cathy did not turn up for her session in September, leaving a message the next day that she had decided to end the therapy. I struggled with not wanting to push against Cathy's autonomy and at the same time knowing that by her own account, she had ended therapy once before just as she was on the threshold of deepening the process. I also knew that something had gone wrong at my end in the two sessions before the break. I recall that my main concern at this time was an ethical one. The ethical code of my professional association, like most, emphasises our respect for the client's "autonomy" and "self determination". Was I riding roughshod over this principle? Could my desire to press Cathy to return to therapy be construed as pushing her in an unacceptable way? I recall being far more worried about the imagined reactions of my peers, rather than any concern about what Cathy might do.

My bedrock question here boiled down to: "Am I proposing to do something in the service of this client's personal development, or not?" The answer then seemed clear. Cathy is a client with a strong schizoid presentation and a chaotic/avoidant attachment history. Cathy herself values "autonomy", or independence, meaning "It's safer not to depend on anyone else, even if this means that I then feel utterly alone and unsupported inside myself". I could decide to stand in the way of her leaving therapy at this point, with the result that she would repeat the experience of the earlier therapeutic encounters that she had terminated too soon. Or I could attempt to support her in trying something a bit different, and ask her to engage with me enough to make a joint decision about the future of her therapy with me. "The client's autonomy does not absolve us therapists of our responsibility to do what we can to challenge our clients to use the therapeutic opportunity fully" (Bugenthal, 1981, p. 198). When I rang her back, Cathy agreed to come at least one more time before she made her final decision.

I did some careful self-examination before we met for this session. First, I understood that Cathy was not withdrawing in order to reject me, but because she found intimacy so threatening. She also seemed to think that her absence would not affect me in the least. I held in my mind that in the problematic sessions before my summer break, Cathy had seemingly evoked my boredom as a way of making sure

I did not get too close. You could say that she re-created her "usual" experience in relationships with others, making me "lose interest" in her. I decided that my first aim in meeting with Cathy was pretty basic: to listen carefully to her reasons for wanting to leave therapy before considering my own response.

Beyond that, there were several things I knew I wanted to share with her, based on my appraisal of work done so far in therapy. My awareness that Cathy had withdrawn from previous therapies when she was approaching more of her core material made me want to challenge this "repeating" of history. The fact of her repeating it suggested to me both her fear of "going deeper", which she was aware of, and a desire–a deep, organismic longing–to do that very familiar thing and to survive on her own. In a trickier vein, I felt the need to bring up the subject of her excluding me from her decision and to see if my hunch was correct, that she thought at some level that I really could not care less. At the same time, I wished to acknowledge her ability to see herself through difficult times on her own, as she had done often in her life so far. As well as this, she and I now had memories of her sharing difficult experiences and feeling my committed support for her in working them through. I thought that Cathy had been helped by me without losing her "independence", but she might not agree, being so sensitised to dependency. It seemed to me, at any rate, that she was considering leaving therapy just at the point where she was also expressing her appreciation of the work so far.

Lastly, as I prepared for this return session, I intended to make it possible for Cathy to disagree, argue and thereby clarify matters with me. Her tendency before the break had been towards a rather idealised view of me. The desire for confluence had influenced the transferential space on both sides, as I could now see. I had been to an extent buying into Cathy's idealised projections. Realising this now helped re-ground me back in my own distinct and separate being, yet with a lot of compassionate and professional concern for this client who was struggling with intimacy.

In the event, during the return session, I felt that this preparation had paid dividends in helping create a good clear space for discussion and negotiation. A key statement for me was Cathy's:

> "Until today, I don't think I ever thought about *our* relationship. Now that I do, I know that you do care about me and that money doesn't cover it. That's my dad talking, when I think like that."

For a moment or two we were silent in acknowledgement of this resting together after effort and I knew things would be OK whatever the final decision. The outcome of our negotiation was that Cathy and I agreed that she would take a "sort of break" from therapy. But would come to see me once a month for three months and then see where she wanted to go from there.

Reconciliation

At the close of the second of these monthly sessions I noted Cathy's comment as she was leaving, "I did think that you might have been annoyed with me before your summer holiday", and made a note to follow this up next time. When we met a month later, Cathy launched straight in to a tale of a disrupted work relationship, where a colleague had not acknowledged Cathy's hello in the morning. I supported her in minutely describing her experience of feeling dismissed, ignored, and worthless yet nevertheless finding the courage to go back and say hello again. The reason Cathy went back was to check, "Did she really ignore me or did I imagine it?" And she wondered, "Can I have another go at making contact with this person?"

I felt immediately that Cathy was seeking such detailed help with this experience because it was depressingly familiar to her. In Gestalt terms, she would often come to the point of fore-contact with loaded expectations of hope, plus a pre-emptive despair of connection. Made sensitive to the merest whiff of rejection, she would swing into withdrawal and self-hurting introspection. Maybe if Cathy could hang around long enough to judge whether the other person did in fact want contact with her, she might experience some satisfaction of her desire before withdrawing.

I also saw Cathy's interest in this experience as directly related to our relationship. Bearing in mind all the things I knew about Cathy's personality style and attachment history, I was very careful, slow and reflective in my response. I told Cathy that I thought she had got so used to managing on what I termed "the pauper's share" of loving contact when she was growing up, that she might have come to blame herself for that, seeing herself as too boring or uninteresting in the eyes of the other, significant person. I understood how one consequence of this experience might be to make it very hard to "try again" with a person, in case they reinforced the message by ignoring her or acting bored. In my heart, I knew that the real story of Cathy's early relationships was far worse than she was aware of. She was indeed a cruelly hated child, from what she had told me about her relational history, but I judged it to be far too early in the therapy for Cathy to consider that. Hence I went on to say,

> "This experience with your work colleague brings my mind back to last month, when you said you'd noticed I might have been annoyed with you. I wonder if you feel able to tell me a little more about that now?"

I was amazed at the clarity and directness of Cathy's reply.

> "Yes–that was really why I thought we'd gone as far as we could go, last summer. That's why I said I wanted to stop."

My amazement rapidly turned to a kind of crystallised, whole body and mind "tuning" to the situation and to Cathy's need within this session. I felt supported by my Gestalt training, which had been about fifty per cent group experience. I could draw with considerable confidence on my ability to support her in criticising me, so that I might then acknowledge my part in creating the experience of rupture in our relationship. I had a strong desire to acknowledge and accept whatever Cathy had to say to me, to see the meaning for her and work it through if possible. Looking back on this, the point for me is that both my Gestalt training, and the insights I had gained from object relations theory into Cathy's schizoid self-process, were necessary for me to support her appropriately. Without Gestalt, I would maybe have been too interpretative and out of personal contact with Cathy. Without an object relations perspective, I could not appreciate the unconscious communication going on. This gave me the sense throughout the exchange that Cathy was simultaneously terrified of having connection with me, because she also wanted to criticise me, and hopelessly-hopefully longed for me to be able to keep connection with her. My understanding of this meant I could tolerate her criticism without retaliating, and in the process diminishing her, or myself, both of which would have left her feeling abandoned again.

All these thoughts and feelings were in my experience as I prepared to listen to her explaining what had worried her last summer. Cathy said,

"You seemed to look past me. People do when they are not interested in me. It was very fleeting. You looked sort of over my
shoulder. Maybe you didn't. I don't know".

I asked her if she could help me by trying to recall when this incident happened. I had a particular session in mind as a possibility
but refrained from suggesting it. I wanted her to feel safe enough to
find out her own awareness, which might anyway not be the same
as mine. This was hard for a while because at first Cathy could not
recall, exactly, so I said,

> "Cathy, I know that you would not be saying I did this unless I
> did. I know sometimes you don't tell me things or might not tell
> the truth straight away if you feel uncomfortable about some-
> thing, but this is different. And I know that when you do speak
> here, you speak with integrity. So I know I must have done
> something, and I really want to know about it."

Cathy was overcome with relief and tears as she told me exactly
when it was that I had looked fed up and bored in the session before
my summer break the year before. She had held all this–probably
mostly out of awareness–for six months. I felt moved by her courage
and persistence. Our dialogue became very slowed down for the
rest of the session, as we took turns in listening and responding. My
apology, when it came, was heartfelt but in no way that I am aware,
placatory or manipulative.

> "If I did this, Cathy, I am very sorry because I would not want to
> look past you in such a way, but I must have done. In fact, I want
> to say it more strongly than that. Not "if", but I *have* done some-
> thing that was not right, not respectful towards you and I am
> sorry."

Through tears and smiles and sighs, Cathy replied,

> "I'm not used to this. No one does what you do, and say they
> believe me. It's always, "I didn't do that. You're imagining it."
> But to hear you say of course you must have done something,
> and that I wouldn't have made it up, something as important as
> this. It's just wonderful."

I think Cathy's original wound had been opened up in that experi-ence of my "looking past her". My willingness to attend to her wound made her self-healing possible. The genuineness of my sor-row conveyed healing without words. This in itself would have been a beautiful experience of dialogic connection and I was half tempt-ed to leave it there, but something still niggled. My belief is that Cathy's schizoid experience has at its heart, not just the terrible despair and longing for connection described so far, but also the belief that her love must be harmful to other people. Why else would Cathy believe that others find the idea of contact and rela-tionship with her so repugnant? I therefore suspected that she would be dealing with the worry that her criticism of me might well destroy me, or at least destroy any future chance of relationship with me. I decided to address this by saying there was something more I wanted to add to my apology. Cathy immediately looked worried and jolted out of her reflections but she asked me to continue.

> "OK", I said, "I want you to know that as well as all the things I've said–I'm sorry and you know that now … as well as that, I want you to know that I do not feel crushed or destroyed by the fact that I did something wrong, and you've helped me to see that and heard my "sorry". I *am* sorry and I've learned a valuable lesson too. I'm reminded that I'm not perfect! Sometimes I forget that I can make mistakes and get things wrong. So I know more clearly than before that I'm not perfect; much as I want to be the "perfect therapist" for you, I can't be. But I do not feel crushed, just newly aware."

Cathy was able to laugh at this point and say, "I can see that!" before raising a worry of her own. "But Patti, will things change between us, now?" Guessing that Cathy meant "change for the worse", I said,

> "Yes, I trust things will change. It might be easier for you in future to tell me nearer the time, if I've upset or worried you, or if you think I'm feeling something that I'm not saying, like being angry or bored."

Surprisingly, Cathy likened this process to the reconciliation talks that were then going on in South Africa.

"This is what people need, isn't it? Forgiveness. But forgiveness kind of flowers of its own accord, when I run the risk, as it feels to me, of blaming you, then you say sorry like I've never heard before. People just need to have their pain and sorrow witnessed. Then forgiveness flowers."

Afterwards, my supervision group helped me see that in saying that I was not crushed after acknowledging my wrongdoing to Cathy, I helped her to see me as a good person who can nevertheless do a bad thing. I had not intended to hurt her but I acknowledged that I had in fact hurt her, and apologised. This restored me as a "good object" without needing to keep me as a "perfect" person. There is more safety in this revised view of our relationship, both for Cathy and myself.

Moving forward

After this episode, we were able to resume weekly therapy for a further fruitful period of 15 months. Therapeutic work in this period was largely life counselling, centring on a better understanding of her relationships, at first within her family of origin, with her four children and latterly with her husband. We also did some tracking of the remaining impact on Cathy's current life of a much disrupted and sometimes chaotic childhood and adolescence. Then there came a planned break of 10 months whilst Cathy took a vocational course, which we both saw as very positive for her as it would lead to work more suited to her capabilities. Cathy was clear then, however, that it was a break and that she would like to return to therapy and work on "deeper" issues she was aware of, which we discussed briefly. We decided to meet during this break for two "check-in" sessions, in order for Cathy to feel she was remaining in contact with me and for us both to review how she was feeling about the break from therapy and her sense of whether she wanted to resume as planned at the end of the period.

At the first of these check-ins Cathy expressed her conflict about wanting to continue with her course, yet being clear about what she would "go on to" in therapy, at some future point. Bearing in mind her tendency to split her experience, combined with the continuing issue about pleasing me versus rejecting me, I asked her to consider if she might not be able to choose one–the course or her therapy–at the moment, without diminishing the other. This seemed to liberate her and we agreed to meet again, after the course finished in five months time, and review the therapy situation then. Cathy's words stuck with me:

> "I'm enjoying the basis we've built. I used to think you should only go to therapy if there's something awfully wrong. But now I know I want to start again later on because you help me with personal stuff that I can't deal with as I want to. You make it easier, whereas I used to think that therapy made it harder."

Cathy has returned to weekly therapy, having completed her qualification. She now says that she wants to work on her feelings of shame about a number of things, including her possibly addictive attitude to alcohol and to relationships, like that with her father, which confusingly involve shame and attraction. In proposing this work, I felt Cathy was also expressing a wish to have more intimacy and trust with me. She confirmed this when I put it to her, saying she felt much easier with me since "that time when you said sorry to me and believed me instead of dismissing me". So that session (now over two years ago) still holds a lot of powerful assurance for her and can be called upon by either of us at times when Cathy feels too frightened of the possible risk of "rupture" to tell me something.

Diagnostic thoughts

Though she rarely expresses the shadow side, preferring usually to present as bright and breezy, at one recent session Cathy came "in a very low state". This centred on her experience of feeling "incredibly lonely ... not wanted by friends or family", and "feeling like an uninvited guest", wherever she went. She knew that she had "driven away" people who would like to be closer to her, including her husband. I will not go into the aspect of our work that has been addressing how Cathy is splitting her relationships and herself in the process, thereby gaining only partial and unfulfilling intimacy, though this has obviously been important. The point I want to make here is that, from an object relations perspective I see Cathy as being depressed at the moment, but in a schizoid rather than narcissistic way, and this is a big influence on the way I am working with her.

Basically, narcissistic depression seems to me to centre on guilt, with the client's "top dog" (Perls, 1951) or superego tormenting her in secret for things she has or has not done. This kind of depression usually relates to experience as a child, where parents do not love the child as a being, but instead give or withhold love as a reward or punishment for achievement or behaviour. Such a person will defend herself by employing the familiar narcissistic means of feeling grandiosely important and/or completely diminished, worthless in relation to others. For a long time, I saw Cathy's episodes of depressive experience in these terms, but I came to see them differently. Heath (1991) puts it this way:

> There is a "schizoid" sense of futility, which at first seems similar to, but which is distinguished from, depression. The sufferer is unable to relate to an internal object. He or she projects representations of this onto an external object or a person, then feels a sense of futility about his or her inability to relate to this other person, or to others. This state is usually chronic and is often confused with chronic depression. [p. 92]

These thoughts were with me in a recent supervision session where I was talking about Cathy's wish to work on shame. My supervisor said in a rather irritated manner,

> "But is it deep shame? Is she suffering? There doesn't seem to be much evidence of this."

I was forced to agree with him from one point of view, for Cathy was not apparently feeling any shame about her continuing to act in ways that exhibited what could be seen as adolescent acting-out behaviour–testing her nice husband by getting drunk, for example.

And yet, I did feel very strongly that Cathy experiences shame of some kind. In my next supervision we explored in more detail my bodily countertransference. Robert Shaw (2003, p. 53) has written that "the response of the therapist is an embodied one" and argues that this needs to be part of the co-construction of a therapeutic narrative. When I allowed my bodily countertransference to emerge, what I got was a kind of falling away lurch, followed by a desperate attempt to right myself. To me this means that when Cathy seeks connection, which she deeply longs for, she experiences *at the same time* this existential bottomless falling into a long continuous dying, but without the finality of death at the end. This I recognise, from my own experience and from that of other clients I have worked with, as the core schizoid experience of relating, or trying to relate. The longing for relationship always goes along with this experience of falling away into nothingness. So I understand Cathy's "depression" to mean recognition of the utter futility, for her, of hoping for an experience of relationship. It is despair of ever satisfying that longed for need of relationship and connection. Part of the awfulness is that when put into words, this despair sounds like, and comes to feel like "depression". ("I feel low in energy, miserable and tearful, empty".) The words cannot capture the internal experience and no words of the therapist can in my opinion fully connect with this. Trying to relate to Cathy in that place of longing and simultaneously falling away, I can only be with her in my imagination, experience, my bodily empathy, my unconsciously communicated attunement. Words that attempt to name her experience can hold her to an extent but they do not relieve her pain in the slightest. Her pain is also excruciatingly shame-full. As she said at one point,

> "I think my need (to relate, connect, have real contact) is actually disgusting. I know this because people cringe when I try to get close to them. Ugh–not her again!"

This understanding of Cathy's work in therapy is now informing my approach. If I am to support her in a deeper recognition and, hopefully, accommodation of her schizoid experience, the seat of her shame-full despair, I need to help us create the optimum therapeutic container. That means building on her so far relatively limited experience of the possibilities for intimacy and mutual trust in our relationship. In practical terms it means making safe time together over an extended period and the continuity of regular weekly, or maybe for periods twice-weekly, meetings. On the other hand, Cathy still has real limitations in tolerating those very things that she needs: intimacy, trust, continuity, committed time together. That is exactly why, up to now, I have gone with her process but also tried to provide enough containment without frightening her too much or making her feel trapped. This has at times included pushing her to consider staying in therapy when she would otherwise have left on a whim, or on the assumption that it would not matter to me if she did leave. At other times it has meant negotiating slowed down periods of therapy, and breaks to reflect and practise, before resuming the therapeutic journey together.

Re-contracting

My sense now, however, is that Cathy can tolerate more explicit reference to this material, namely hers and my relationship, and the therapeutic endeavour as it is contained within a therapeutic frame. This is why, since re-starting weekly therapy, a part of the work has been a special kind of "re-contracting". My aim is to have written down in our therapy agreement not just the standard things that Cathy has signed up to before, as do all my clients, about fees, time-keeping and so on, but also some words to represent special issues of agreement that are quite personal and particular to Cathy and me during this next period of therapy. It is not unusual for me to discuss or review a period of therapy, before moving on to new areas of enquiry with any client, but there are particular reasons why I want to get things on paper with her.

First, I think that it will help her to have a concrete record summarising the agreement we have reached on issues she and I want to address next; something for her to hold on to when she feels the world–and me with it–sliding away. Secondly, and just as importantly, I want to ensure as far as possible that, should Cathy reach another point where she can not tolerate the disappointment of her hopes for relationship with me, after I maybe have upset her, pushed her too hard, or alternatively made her feel abandoned to that "falling" place, I will be able to remind her that this is an experience we both thought she might have, something we thought might happen. She can have a choice then, for example, about whether to miss a session or not, to go on with therapy or not. She can go on with her old view of relationship, or she can remember that she has experienced me staying with her and being prepared to listen and talk things through. This makes more sense to me of the notion of Cathy taking "responsibility", because it recognises both her difficulties and her current options, which are also affected by the responsibility I take as her therapist. In one sense, all this is to protect me a bit from the possibility of complaint in the future, though in reality I do not fear Cathy doing that. Even so, it seems to me to be useful practice. In another sense, I help provide a surer and more grounded therapeutic container for Cathy because I am willing to prepare explicitly for eventualities that might happen with me, and that she experiences daily in other relationships in her life.

The first thing that happened when Cathy returned as planned to weekly therapy was that she "forgot" to turn up. When we met the following week, we agreed that we would re-contract over the coming weeks, making a personalised therapy agreement as I have described, focusing on the issues she wanted to work on and thoughts about how best to make a "container" for that work. Cathy had come to the session saying "I know what I want to work on–my experiences of feeling disgusting and shameful. My experiences of pain and pleasure are so inter-related". I noted the content of her words but felt unwilling to launch into discussion right then. Instead, we discussed the issue of her "forgetting" to come the previous week. We agreed that this indicated at the least ambivalence, and probably the opposite of being keen to work on these shaming issues. Cathy said then that she felt afraid of coming back into regular weekly therapy with me and in the process facing the prospect of trying to relate to me as well as exposing more of her uncomfortable inner world.

Since then nearly every weekly session has in some way addressed the split between Cathy's wish to go on with the work as planned and at the same time her fear or ambivalence about actually making a containing contract with me. My response has been to work quite light-handedly with the issues Cathy brings, whilst also ensuring we spend a little bit of time each week on finding the right words for our contract, or "therapy agreement" as we call it. This is how it is shaping up.

The first clause we inserted reflects the experience, some two or more years earlier, of working through the rupture of relationship caused by my "looking over Cathy's shoulder". Cathy suggested it and we worded it jointly, evoking an appreciation of what we had been through and Cathy's statement that it was "good to have this on our agreement as a reminder".

Cathy has felt an underlying anxiety about re-connecting with Patti in case Patti gets bored or angry with her. Both Cathy and Patti therefore undertake to say, if we can, our awareness of this happening. Cathy will try to tell Patti if she feels Patti is bored or angry (or anything else she thinks Patti is feeling or thinking at the time which is interfering with her therapy work). Cathy will say if she is feeling bored or angry herself. Patti will tell Cathy if she is bored or angry, as long as Patti is clear that she is not bored or angry on her own account, but genuinely as a result of something that is happening between Cathy and Patti.

Another session focused on Cathy's "spoiler" sub-personality; the one who calls her a failure or an uninteresting person and in the process undermines her relationships. Cathy explored how "forgetting" sessions or arriving late induced the "spoiler" to say that I would get fed up with her. When Cathy checked this out with me, she was reminded that "forgetting" was not a failure, so much as an expression of her fearfulness which co-exists with her longing for safe connection with me. Cathy said, "This feels like the first time I am taking responsibility for our relationship". On our new contract this is expressed as follows:

Both Cathy and Patti have responsibilities in this relationship. Sometimes Cathy will be aware of her responsibility. At other times, Patti will take her responsibility. At other times, responsibility will be negotiated and shared. Both Cathy and Patti are part of this ebb and flow, but Patti has a particular responsibility to try and name what might be happening in the therapeutic relationship and help Cathy feel safe and fully able to do her work. For her part, Cathy wants to try to remember times when she and Patti have worked through things that have made Cathy feel worried or annoyed or feeling as if Cathy is to blame in some way. Cathy will speak as soon as she can, if such matters arise again, knowing that Patti is willing to work it through together.

In another session, we had been looking at how Cathy's early attachment experiences might have influenced her development, especially her experiences of connection and abandonment. I had initially introduced this topic rather as if I were teaching her something about all human beings, to see if she liked the theory as it might apply to herself. We had been talking about Cathy's long, drawn out, childhood experiences of repeated separation from her mother, interspersed with time spent in the care of a hateful father who projected his own unwanted psychological material onto her. Cathy was wondering how this early attachment and separation experience might sometimes be re-activated in her current relationships, recalling her recent annoyance when her husband called her mobile phone to ask "Where are you?"

I suggested we experiment with these words. Cathy first said them to her mother, represented by the back of an armchair. "Where are you mum?" turned quickly into a distressed "Where am I? I am lost, hopeless. There's nothing. A hollow hole. I cannot bear this". Cathy had made contact with her feelings of being abandoned in her hopeless search for an internally experienced "mother". Despite her upset, Cathy robustly suggested trying out saying these words to her father, represented by a huge pile of cushions. "Where are you. You're bloody hiding. I know you don't want me, so why do you ask me where I am? I can't stand you calling me–invading my private space. Go away! I don't want you!"

This work led to the inclusion of another point on our new contract:

> We both know that Cathy's experiences of early attachment–being sometimes connection, sometimes invasion, sometimes abandonment–can get activated in relationships here and now. Cathy wants to learn more about this and Patti will help her to notice when these old patterns are making an appearance in Cathy's current experience. It is important to remember that this process of re-activating familiar attachment patterns is not "failure" but something that happens in all human beings. We will need to be loving and compassionate to Cathy as she does this work.

In yet another session I noticed aloud that Cathy seemed to me to be very hungry for my contributions that day. I felt, but did not say, that it was as if she wanted to swallow my food whole, rather than chew it first. This might provide food of a kind for that empty schizoid core (Seinfeld, 1990) but I did not want to "clog her up" with introjected material either. The new contract reflects this in saying:

> Patti is willing to share with Cathy her expertise as a psychotherapist and any relevant fruits of her experience as an older woman. Cathy is willing to use and share her own unique expertise on her self. Cathy will try to tell Patti if she thinks Patti is wrong, or if Cathy disagrees on some point, or does not see the relevance. Cathy understands that

Patti does not consider it a failure if she is seen as wrong or misun-
derstood. Cathy knows from experience that Patti is not perfect or
anywhere near it. Patti wants to know these things just as much as
the times when Cathy is pleased or helped by a contribution from
Patti.

Most recently, Cathy and I have been looking again at the meaning of "forgetting" sessions. What does it mean to Cathy that we have an arrangement where if necessary I will ring her to remind her? What would it mean to stop this arrangement? Does her willing payment for missed sessions give her the freedom to "forget", in the context of imagining that I don't care as long as I get her money? If forgetting means "failing", how should we address this pattern of behaviour in future? Following a recent discussion with my peer supervision group I suspect that this issue may connect directly with Cathy's own stated issues. It seems likely that Cathy "forgets" to come to therapy when she feels shamed, either by some overt action of hers, or even by a shameful thought, such as wishing she were going to see her pub friends and not me, her therapist. Contractually, I hope we can now revise the arrangement whereby I sometimes remind her with a prompting phone call. It seems time for her to take the responsibility for remembering if she can. I hope to find words that will acknowledge her difficulty and yet state an expectation that Cathy will notice her "forgetting" in a way that takes into account her own therapeutic awareness. If she forgets, I hope she will be able to address this in the therapy in a way she would not have been able to in previous years. In terms of the deeper work on shame and schizoid repair, this might support Cathy's experience of personal success and her sense of fuller relationship with me.

With Cathy's agreement, I am noting these contractual points for discussion week by week. So far, I see the re-contracting exercise as complementary to the work of returning to therapy, for Cathy. She talks now of "our personal agreement" and seems genuinely delighted that we are creating a contract that is special to her and me. In the process, I feel that together we are making a surer container for the therapeutic work that lies ahead.

CHAPTER SIX

Where there's smoke there's fire

Theresa Bernier and Anne Kearns

Theresa had a complaint made against her through the BACP by a former client who had ended the therapy abruptly a year earlier. This is Theresa's account of her experience, with some factual amendments that belong to other people's stories that I've *(AK)* made in order to protect Theresa's anonymity and that of her former client. The story is interspersed and supported by my comments, which are drawn from interviews with others who have been through complaints procedures, my own and their correspondence with the BACP and several visits to the British Library, particularly to wade through the relevant parts of recent (2002–06) issues of the *Counselling and Psychotherapy Journal* and its successor, *Therapy Today*.

Background

(TR) Tamara was referred to me by my supervisor when I was in the final year of my training in Person Centred counselling. I went on to train in a more psychodynamic psychotherapeutic approach and Tamara continued in therapy with me throughout that training. We worked together for nearly five years. She had come to therapy initially at the urging of her then partner who, Tamara said, thought she was "mental" and needed help. Tamara told me that she had difficulty containing her anger and was sometimes violent with her partner, which she linked to her having grown up in a household where father was often drunk and physically abusive and mother passive and compliant. Although I would not learn until a few months later that Tamara's pattern in life was to defend against others' perceived failures by making both formal and informal complaints against colleagues, employers and various professionals, she did tell me in that first session that she often felt picked on and that she believed things went wrong for her in a way that they did not go wrong for others. She said her car never worked properly, household appliances broke down and she was often unwell herself, suffering from a series of ailments, including osteoarthritis. She was also on several medications, which she had been prescribed to help her combat pain. Among this list were at least two medicines widely known to be addictive and to result in mood swings and unpleasant side effects of withdrawal. Weeks later she would also admit to self-harm.

During that first session she said she suffered from terrible "waking nightmares" where she became anxious that she was dead. Five years earlier she had been referred to a psychiatrist after losing her job close after the break-up of a relationship caused her to "shut down". Following an assessment the psychiatrist had suggested group therapy but Tamara had been horrified at the idea and had declined to take up the offer of a weekly place. She said the psychiatrist didn't really know what he was talking about.

I liked Tamara. She was feisty and funny. Humour was an important factor in how we related to each other in the early days of therapy and, interestingly, even at the end.

The supervisor who referred Tamara to me was seeing her brother for therapy. When I suggested that Tamara might be better served by working with someone more experienced than myself, my supervisor said, "You need to cut your teeth somewhere", suggesting that, just because Tamara might be difficult to work with, this was not a sufficient reason to refer her on.

Boundary issues

Very little attention was paid in my counselling training to the concept of boundaries. As you can see my supervisor felt fine about referring Tamara to me, even though he was seeing her brother. At the time I didn't foresee that as a problem. I realise now that even before meeting Tamara a professional boundary had been crossed. I was aware, though, in the first supervision session after I started seeing Tamara, that my supervisor asked me a question that he would never have asked had he not had information from his client about my client. Eventually I was able to drum up the courage to challenge my supervisor's occasional slips and to take Tamara to another supervisor who was more psychoanalytically informed and where there were no boundary issues.

Transference issues

My new supervisor helped me to see that in my eagerness to be a "good counsellor" and through my naïveté in overlooking who I might come to represent in the transference–either the abusive father or the passive mother who betrayed Tamara through their failures to protect her–I had not prepared myself for what would happen when Tamara felt close enough to me to re-enact her rage at the abuse she suffered as a child. These terrible and dramatic aspects of her childhood were rarely acknowledged in words in our work together, but I came to see how they were being re-enacted in the transference. As I became more sophisticated as a practitioner and more in tune with the transference and countertransference playing out between us, Tamara became more resistant to the therapy. The further away I moved from my humanistic roots with a clinical emphasis on the core conditions (Rogers, 1951) and began to make interpretations and to challenge Tamara's thinking she became enraged. My supervisor supported me to make a specific contract with Tamara that she and I would stay in the relationship through difficult times and that she would not leave without planning an ending.

I do think it is also important to stress that these were not five years of unmitigated therapeutic failure. Tamara did begin to recognise that her rages against her neighbours, colleagues and friends were often out of proportion to current events and were inevitably sparked by connecting with traumatic elements in her past. Tamara was even able to contain her rage at times and for a full three years she did not take out any grievances at work. She no longer participated in dangerous sexual activities and I believe she also began to appreciate the containment my boundaries provided her; her sessions began and ended on time. Despite her rages I did not retaliate, shout, leave the room or throw her out as she often expected I would. Tamara's was a history without consistency or restraint, and I believe I did provide her with that.

A rupture

Our work together ended abruptly after five years. I had taken a three-week Christmas break after which Tamara phoned to say she was ill and unable to attend her sessions for several weeks. The day before she was to return I had a family bereavement and I was forced to cancel my work for two weeks. When I returned Tamara was furious. I had told her that there had been both a family crisis and a bereavement, though she was so enraged by my absence that she did not appear to hear me. She felt abandoned and frustrated that I would not tell her in more detail why I had been forced to cancel her sessions.

Throughout the years I worked with Tamara I was careful not to reveal details concerning my personal life because I believed it was more helpful to discuss who and what she imagined me to be in the transference. It was through her projections on to me that I believed and still believe, we were able to make some sense of her earlier experiences and to understand how they influenced her current relationships.

Even though I *had* given Tamara the reasons for my unplanned absence her anxiety was such that she could not take in the information. We looked at this on my return but she experienced my refusal to give her any more details as withholding and infuriating. She had always experienced my breaks as abandonment and, just as she had done after my Christmas break, she often found ways not to attend her sessions following my return. This time I had been forced to cancel just at the point when she felt safe enough to return. By returning to therapy on her terms she felt she was in control of events, again managing in the present what could not be controlled in her childhood—abuse and abandonment. In essence, I believe I became the abandoning mother in the transference. So, in another effort to regain control, she abandoned me. Tamara announced that she was ending the therapy in three weeks time. In the middle of the final session she simply stood up and walked out with the parting shot, "I hope you're happy!"

When I heard nothing more from her I wrote to her to say I was sorry that she hadn't felt able to stay and work through what had made her leave the last session abruptly and that I very much hoped that she would feel able to come back to see me at least one more time and to honour the contract we had made.

I never heard from her again. A year passed. I hoped, of course, that I would be the exception to her rule that anyone who was perceived to have let her down deserved to be complained against. I told myself that, despite the abrupt and un-worked-through ending, she *had* benefited from the therapy after all. I even convinced myself that Tamara not taking out a complaint against me was evidence of this. Now I know that this was simply an extension of the naïveté that had led me to take on this client in the first place and to persist with the relationship when I knew that, given her history, she would need to attack me in order to take revenge, but also to stay connected to me and feel in control. As Benjamin (1996) points out, those people who have suffered abuse in their childhood often alternate between seduction and attack. Seduction creates the illusion of intimacy but also sparks an unconscious memory of the original trauma, leading to attack. I believe Tamara was enraged because she *could not* seduce me, even as my giving in to her would have also provoked profound rage. I could not win.

During the years that I worked with Tamara my supervisor and colleagues regularly raised the possibility of onward referral. I felt caught between a rock and a hard place. Knowing that Tamara had been yet unable to work through her abandonment terrors and defensive rage I knew that it was likely that she would see onward referral, even if it was in her best interest and explained compassionately, as a rejection. That she would put down to my failure. I also knew that, even if I kept working with her in the hope that I could contain the negative transference and work through her history of abuse, the relationship could break down at any moment. Either way I would be likely to have a complaint taken out against me. When, at a time when Tamara was in great distress and unable to go to work, I did, gently, suggest a psychiatric assessment she became enraged, asking me over and over again if I thought she was crazy. When I helped her to consider other kinds of therapy that might put less emphasis on linking the past to the present such as CBT, she was very clear that she thought that I was the therapist for her, saying that we already had a relationship and that I knew her well enough not to let her "get away with anything".

With hindsight I realise that I was also afraid that I would be seen by my colleagues and supervisor and Tamara as failing her by referring her on. I used to spend hours outside the therapy asking myself if I was just scared and shirking my duty, opting out simply because the going got too tough while at the same time knowing that of course it was bound to get tough. Indeed, Tamara and I did have a good deal of experience of doing good work when things got tough. So, in the end, I hung in there.

The complaint

Nothing in my training, or my history, prepared me for the experience of having a complaint made against me. Only the niggling fear throughout my work with this client that one day this *could* happen forced me to consider in the back of my mind how I would cope if it did. The letter giving me notice that the BACP had received a complaint from my former client arrived by special delivery, in a letter marked "confidential". It was in an innocuous envelope I assumed contained a credit card. The initial correspondence said a complaint had been lodged and was being investigated. They explained that a panel would convene (apparently without speaking to me) and decide whether or not there was, *prima facie*, a case to answer. The letter from the BACP said that "you are not required to respond at this stage, but you will be given an opportunity at a later stage if the complaint is accepted".

I felt shocked and very concerned–not just about my own safety and professional reputation–but also about Tamara. I could not see how this process could hold her enough, knowing that her story alone would be the basis on which the "pre-hearing assessment panel" made their decision. I believed that as her therapist I had some responsibility to ensure that she and I could meet with some assistance to unpick what had caused her to take this action. I rang the BACP for clarification about the phrase "you are not required to respond at this stage". They told me that it actually meant that they were not going to consider *any* response from me or from my supervisor unless the decision was made to move to a full hearing. I felt kicked in the gut. I couldn't understand how a panel could make this decision based solely on whatever information they had from Tamara. At this stage I had not seen the content of her complaint and knew nothing of the charges.

I was surprised and confused that the BACP were proceeding to the "screening" stage at all. Their Professional Conduct Procedure states clearly that a person making a complaint "is expected to attempt to resolve the issue with the individual or organisational Member Complained Against. The Complainant must demonstrate that all informal channels have been exhausted".

Tamara had not even tried, let alone "exhausted" informal channels! She had stormed out of a session, didn't reply to my letter and I heard nothing further from her for over a year until I received the letter from the BACP.

After a month I received a letter from the BACP letting me know that the complaint had been considered by their Pre-Hearing Assessment Panel who had decided that there was "a case to answer". They went on to say: "While the Panel was concerned with the allegations made in the complaint as a whole, the Panel had additional particular concerns with regard to the principle of autonomy". I felt at once concerned and relieved. I reckoned that their concern with the principle of autonomy had to do with my strongly urging Tamara in the letter I wrote to her to come back into therapy to sort things out.

(AK) The BACP maintain that the job of the screening or "Pre-Hearing Assessment Panel" is not to form an opinion about either party, rather to make a decision as to whether or not the complaint should proceed to adjudication. I and others do not see how that is possible to do without some sort of dialogue with both parties and, where appropriate, the supervisor. The BACP seem to be omitting a critical stage in the process of discovery leaving the screening panel to make a decision that profoundly effects the life and relational field of both the complainant and the person complained against with only half of the information that could be available to them.

(TR) In the weeks between when I received the letter and the panel met to make their decision, I dared to hope. I told myself that the panel members would be able to see clearly that this was not a complaint based on evidence of professional misconduct but rather that something had been awakened in the transference that belonged back in the consulting room or, at least in a forum that could support mediation.

A few weeks letter I received word that the complaint was to go to a full hearing on a date set nearly four months away. The document setting out the details of Tamara's complaint was huge, or at least it seemed so to me. It was also clearly drawn up by a lawyer. This was not a complaint accusing me of sexual misconduct, exploitation, corrupt behaviour, or boundary infringement, but rather a ten-page document outlining my client's unhappiness with the manner in which the therapeutic relationship ended. I contacted the BACP and asked them what they would advise.

It is difficult now to convey just how unhelpful the BACP was towards me. Since I first rang asking for help I have spoken to many others who have had the same experience. They share my concern that there is no system in place to provide support other than the feeble offering of telephone contact with others who are undergoing the same trauma. They do not provide a representative to advise or support you, unlike other professional organisations such as the BPS or the GMC do under similar circumstances, nor do they provide legal or practical guidance on how to respond to the complaint other than to give the remarkable advice that calling on a lawyer might not be helpful! Their reasoning was that this might escalate the proceedings. In light of the fact that Tamara had obviously had help from a lawyer in formulating her complaint I found this advice to be astonishingly inept and potentially damaging.

I did not want the offer of telephone peer support from my professional organisation, I wanted information. I had three weeks to write my first rebuttal of the charges laid against me. I still felt concerned about what it might mean to Tamara's mental health to face me in a tribunal and phoned the BACP one more time to check if there was anyway an "informal" meeting could be arranged. The person I spoke to firmly replied, "You've left it a little late for that". I had a similar feeling in my body as I had when Tamara strode out of what was to be our last session.

The BACP say that it is not their role to support mediation between the parties to a complaint, saying, rather, that seeking mediation is the responsibility of the complainant! When I asked if I could approach my client to meet informally they said that that was not possible as a formal complaint had already been made, or words to that effect. Apparently one of their earlier complaints procedures did contain a formal mediation stage yet, according to a colleague who had a conversation with someone at the BACP, parties to complaints were already entrenched in their positions and didn't seem to want to pursue it. It seems to me that it is exactly because parties to complaints *do* become entrenched in their views (I did, particularly in the early days of receiving news that a complaint had been made against me) that mediation should be the first stage in all complaints not involving serious professional misconduct such as sexual abuse and fraud.

I want to be clear here that clients who have been abused by their therapists certainly deserve a means by which they can gain a hearing and therapists must be held to account for their actions. I also believe my client had a right to register her complaint. My point is that I also had a right to be supported and, at the very least, I deserved to have my professional body provide me with good, practical information on how I should fight my corner.

Containment

Like the aftermath of an accident, it can take some time for the shock to lift and the pain to set in. I felt numb after receiving notice that the complaint was to go to a full hearing, but I was not incapacitated. During that short period I was at least able to take some practical steps. I knew from experience that this emotional paralysis was only temporary and I needed to act fast.

In the first instance I rang my therapist with whom I had ended only a few months before and asked if we could resume our sessions. I knew dealing with this complaint was likely to awaken archaic issues for me and I needed her help to make sense of some of my responses. I also needed her to catch and contain my rage and grief and, most importantly, my terror. By the time I finished leaving my message for her to call me I was gagging with the struggle to keep from crying. Already the numbness was wearing off and a range of emotions that seemed in my more rational moments out of all proportion to the "danger" of the actual situation began to take grip. I also contacted my supervisor and other colleagues who had supported me during my work with this client and were aware that she might take out a complaint. I knew I would need their help and support even more over the following months.

I soon discovered that my professional indemnity insurance was not going to be useful to me as this was not a civil case but rather a professional grievance.(I understand that this has now changed and that most insurers do provide a certain amount of support at this stage). My insurers asked that I send them a copy of the complaint, after which I heard nothing further from them. I understand that others have been given a number for a "legal help-line", funded by the insurers, which has been of varying degrees of assistance, but not even this was offered to me.

I have a very close friend from childhood who is a barrister. If this had not been the case I am sure the whole process would have cost me thousands of pounds in legal fees. I sent him the complaint and he emailed back, "This complaint has been drawn up by someone, probably a lawyer, with experience in litigation. It actually says very little, though he or she has made it go a long way. You're dealing with someone who is practised at drawing up complaints out of nothing. I don't think your former client has a hope in hell but you're going to have to respond to each statement". I was both reassured and terrified. I knew I would have help drawing up my response, but I was terrified of the emotional cost of my client's attack as well as of the potential damage that my "defence" would have on Tamara.

I did all of this in the first two days. I also came to the decision that I would be open about the fact that a complaint had been taken out against me by a former client. I would not breach confidentiality or in anyway disclose inappropriately, but I would not hide from my friends and colleagues. I knew that if I kept it to myself it would become a secret about which I would feel increasingly and unhelpfully ashamed.

Shame

To say that my being accused of unethical behaviour was deeply shameful to me is an understatement. In my darker moments I believed that I had so obviously failed with Tamara and that that failure was going to be made public, even though I knew that the details of the complaint were such that, when seen in context, would not amount to unethical behaviour. But then I worried that allowing Tamara to experience a re-play of old battles in meeting me in a kind of court room, particularly one in which I believed she would see me as "winning", would be unethical. Either way I believed that I would somehow be seen as having failed. I also knew that there were no guarantees that I would be exonerated. Having my friend the barrister on my side was a comfort, but I also knew that justice can be a fickle thing and I could end up with sanctions being imposed and with my name and details of those sanctions being published in the CPJ for all to see. On really bad days I felt like all the world would have a front row seat to watch the proceedings.

I also knew that, while many people supported me, others would also suspect that *something* must have happened for this to occur. In other words, "there's no smoke without fire". How could they not wonder, when in my heart I also feared that this was true?

Personal life

The stress of dealing with the complaint extended, of course, into my personal life. Preparing to write this I asked my partner how he had experienced me during that period. He thought for a few moments and then said, "You were very low and pre-occupied. You were very difficult to get close to because you just couldn't shake it, even for short periods of time. You went on and on how this could be the end of your career, how you'd worked so hard to get to this point and now it might be taken away from you. And that holiday in Asia was terrible".

And it *was* horrible. For three weeks I was in a completely different environment but I still couldn't get rid of the fear, the knowledge that when I got back to England I would be facing the same complaint, the same threat to my professional integrity and my career. I began to consider how I would manage closing my practice, what I would do as an alternative profession. I began preparing for the worst, which seemed, in my traumatised mind the only way to survive this ordeal.

Like an animal concerned with survival and turned in on itself, I was completely self-absorbed during those months. I found it almost impossible to keep my partner in mind, to take into consideration how he might be feeling. I know he worked very hard to make life as comfortable as possible for me, to listen and to encourage me. I became enraged whenever he tried to temper my negative thinking. Focusing on a positive outcome would do me no good at all, I pointed out, particularly if at the end of all this I was sanctioned.

Along with my friend the barrister, my partner believed he could recognise the insubstantial nature of the complaint. But I became concerned that the legal document presented by Tamara was sufficiently well-structured that, if only to avoid a legal hit themselves, the BACP might well have thought it best to take the complaint further and do everything by the book. I even began to fear that, given Tamara's history, the hearing panel would find some way to sanction me to avoid being the subject of a complaint themselves.

I knew that in the sub-text of Tamara's complaint against me the entire story of her own struggle for survival in the face of a sadistic and often drunk father and an inconsistent, complicit and passive mother was written. So was her need to seek revenge on the one hand and to turn me into a better "parent" on the other. I tried hard to hold on to my compassion, even as I tried to work through and survive my own rage. I did not always succeed, but I know that I tried.

Reflections on the therapy

As I have written above I went on to train as a psycho-dynamic psychotherapist two years into my work with Tamara. In hindsight I can see that, after a few years of relative peace, the more I became interested in the dynamics of transference and countertransference the more some of my interventions began to invite fury in the session or acting out between sessions. I remembered how Tamara raged at me for weeks when I would not tell her when my birthday was, loudly letting me know that I was not really interested in her and uncaring. I did not tell her my birthday because I believed she was linking me with her father in the transference at that point. *His* birthday was in August. So is mine. To tell her so would, I believe, have been further proof to her that I was just like him and would have disrupted the possible therapeutic benefits of working through the transference. I asked her instead to tell me when she imagined my birthday was, and of course it was August. My countertransference also warned me of Tamara's desire to invade my world and become like me. She began to dress not unlike I dressed; she even told me she had bought a lamp like the one in my consulting room to put by her bedside. I struggled with the need to retain my separateness and to hold her archaic feelings and beliefs. To be honest, I felt a bit stalked.

There had been times during our work, particularly in the last two years, when I had felt so attacked that I had had to cling to the sides of my chair and keep my feet firmly on the floor to prevent myself from retaliating. I knew that I *had* retaliated at times. I did not shout but I'm sure that some of my interventions had had a pointed edge, more in the spirit of self-defence than to heighten Tamara's awareness of the process. As is true with other clients with Tamara's history of emotional and physical abuse my breaks were experienced by her as abandonment. So were my occasional lapses in understanding and forgetfulness. Not remembering someone's name or getting a sequence of events out of sync would often result in an attack from Tamara. I was experienced as cruel and withholding when I would not give in to her demands that I provide her with information about my history and my personal life. In light of preparing for the hearing I also had to consider in some depth those interventions or unconscious processes that evoked something in her history, or in mine, that we had never managed to think about or work through in this difficult therapeutic relationship. Eventually I felt compassion for Tamara and for myself, knowing that I had done my level best to support her to stay and work things through with me and that, of course, she felt as though I didn't really care about her (One of her allegations was that I only wanted her to continue in therapy for the money). That was on a good day. On bad days, of course, I believed I was as guilty as charged.

Work with clients

I wonder how effective I was as a therapist during that period? How deeply could I allow myself to work when I was in such a state of personal distress? I have to say that I found working with clients a relief. During those fifty minutes I could usually forget what was otherwise the loneliest and most traumatic period of my fifty years. Even profound grief after the death of someone I have loved has always been tinged with the satisfaction that there was value in our contact, that over the years something powerful and good had passed between us, even in the most difficult relationships. In this case there was only a struggle for life, for survival–mine and Tamara's—or at least that is what it often felt like for me.

I continued to work, even taking on new clients. However, it was during this period that I saw two potential clients whom I did refer on to other therapists or services. One client presented with a history of abandonment and an obviously attacking streak that actually frightened me. It was the first time in my years as a therapist that I experienced a frisson of personal fear during the assessment session. I realised how I had not allowed myself to have access to a healthy, diagnostic fear in the past, letting my well-meaning zeal to understand and help people blind me to the fact that not everybody *can* be helped. The other prospective client spoke to me of a history that indicated that in our work together she would probably need to rubbish me. At the time I thought I simply did not have the energy to work this through with her.

I had a full client load and I was not in a position to refer on those clients who were in the middle of their therapy and working through their difficult feelings with me in the transference. I still do not know how well, or how badly, I worked during that period. Did I try to defuse the transference when it became difficult? Probably. Did I avoid what is so important in our work as therapists, allowing my clients to let me feel what they have split off and disowned in order to help them to re-own them and re-live them with me ? No. If anything I felt those things more intensely. How afraid was I that what I believed should be contained within the therapy room might extend into the external world and return as an attack? Very. How often did I work from a defensive position, and how often do I work defensively now, a legacy from that period? Probably, to some extent, most of the time.

The end?

Two days before the hearing was scheduled to take place I received a phone call telling me that Tamara had dropped the charges. Of all the options that occurred to me this had not been one. I thought about this further and realised that she had often taken grievances up to the final hurdle before backing down. The "pleasure" for her was in the wearing down, the fantasy of the other suffering. Like the raging baby attacking the mother, she also needed me to survive the attack. And I did survive, albeit with a need for closure that stays with me.

One way I believed I might get some closure was to write an article for the CPJ about my experience. I did this and submitted it to them, receiving a reply–almost by return of post–that the BACP has a policy of not publishing letters or other accounts by a member complained against as to do so would be to show bias. I felt as though I had important feedback for the organisation as well as for the membership and wrote again saying this. Again, I felt silenced, just as I and others who are complained against are silenced from the outset when our experience of the therapy is not taken into account by the screening panel.

(AK) In my interviews with people who have been through BACP complaints procedures all had similar concerns to those expressed in "Theresa's" story: that the CPJ was not willing to publish their experience of being complained against; that transferential dynamics are not taken seriously enough, leaving difficulties that arise in the therapy to be played out in the complaint rather than supporting both parties to a complaint to meet and to work things through. People who had been exonerated expressed real concern that their former clients had been damaged by the experience of having "lost" at the hearing. One told me that, although he had been found to have behaved within the ethical framework and was exonerated, his former client was considering taking a civil action against him. This would seem to me to signal that these quasi-judicial encounters are not in the least conclusive or helpful.

The people interviewed were also concerned that a pre-hearing assessment panel makes a judgement about whether there is, *prima facie*, a case to answer and so to proceed to a hearing without interviewing the person complained against. All were also concerned that there seemed to be no understanding that the practitioner in these complaints is also vulnerable and has different but not lesser needs for support and safety than the client.

In 2002 The BACP adopted a new "Ethical Framework" based on principles, which replaced its previous, rule-based Code of Ethics. In the October 2003 issue of the CPJ the BACP began its new policy of publishing chapter and verse of complaints that have been upheld. A letter in the next issue expressed shock at the "cruel punishment that the professional conduct procedure now includes this parade of these individuals mistakes"(p. 11). The December issue included an article by Graine Griffin, Chair of the Professional Conduct Committee, explaining that the new policy was a reflection of the desire for transparency in light of the new Ethical Framework, stressing too that reporting the details of a complaint was of educational value. "We all", she wrote, "learn from our mistakes and none of us are [sic] perfect. That is what makes us human beings"(p. 56).

If the published letters are a good indicator of the reaction of the membership to the new policy of naming and shaming it would seem that there is very little support for it. In August 2004, responding to a letter from a concerned member who equated the policy of publishing a lengthy summary of complaints with putting the practitioner in the "stocks"(p. 45), Griffin again defended its educative function, saying that publishing the content of complaints will stem a tendency for readers to fantasise about and exaggerate the nature of complaints and will also enable clients or potential clients to carry out a risk assessment. She also thinks that the BACP's reporting of more than just the codes transgressed allows the public to carry out their own "risk assessment" to decide for themselves if the matter upheld has relevance to the practitioner's work with clients. She believes that this transparency meets with the legal requirement to publish decisions, even claiming that "all professional bodies report the full findings in their own journals"(p. 47). At the time of writing this is not true of the UKCP or their member organisations.

I would argue that, although transparency is a worthy principle, it needs to be held alongside other equally worthy principles such as practitioner self-interest. The detail published in the CPJ (now called, *Therapy Today*) borders on the sadistic, inviting voyeurism and defensiveness rather than reflective learning. Surely the "reporting" requirement was met by the BACP's former policy of publishing the findings of adjudication hearings and by listing any sanctions or suspensions. And surely they could fulfil an educative function by publishing the sort of complaints that they are receiving, including outlining those that are not taken to adjudication as well as those that are without humiliating practitioners who have made mistakes. I am reminded of Sivyer's (2000) article in *Self and Society* where he expressed concern that complaints procedures were taking on the attitude of public flogging. In the light of the BACP's current policy this seems sadly prophetic. Sivyer wrote that, "invariably ... the observer ... becomes judge and jury, criticising sometimes unmercifully and with little if any evidence of either compassion or humility–sometimes even pillorying the therapist complained against" (p. 15).

Neither I nor any of the people I spoke to whose experience and views are expressed here want to give the impression that the BACP's (and other organisations') desire to protect the public is not a worthy and necessary aim. What does concern me is that in their desire to protect the public they have lost sight of the need to support–and in some cases protect–their members.

In 2000 Bond proposed that two additional principles should be added to the four key ethical principles–respect for the client's autonomy,[1] beneficence, non-maleficence and justice–that are commonly called upon to govern ethical practice in counselling and psychotherapy. These are the principles of fidelity and practitioner's self-interest. BACP has incorporated "fidelity" or the need to honour commitments, to its new (2002) Ethical Framework but has substituted "practitioner self-respect" for self-interest. "Self-respect" in this context centres around the practitioner's responsibility to seek professional support and engage in life-enhancing activities. Whereas I believe that this is essential I do not think "self-respect" as understood by the BACP goes far enough to support the practitioner.

Of course our duty of care means that many ethical decisions are made for the good of the client without relevance to the self-interest of the practitioner. The decision not to take on a client because of a possible boundary crossing or to make an onward referral must be made despite, for example, the loss of income or potential income to the therapist. And the principle of self-interest on its own could lead to a therapist taking an adversarial position against a former client. This is not an unlikely as I might have thought five years ago as I know of two practitioners who have had to take out restraining orders against clients who have been stalking them. When held in tandem with the therapist's commitment to honour what she has undertaken (fidelity), to not do harm (non-maleficence) and to promote the client's well-being, and when supported by a process that encourages dialogue as opposed to polarisation, the principle of practitioner self-interest means communicating from the outset that *both* client and therapist have needs for respect and safety. For example, it is ordinarily not in my best interest to be available to answer the phone in the middle of the night. I need to monitor my own self-care, which might mean that I take an unplanned break in order to resource myself.

More than one member complained against expressed concern that their vulnerability was not taken into account, particularly the possibility that, in making a formal complaint, the complainant could be seeking revenge against a past abuser (s) through attacking the therapist. I would challenge the appropriateness of the notion of equality because the complainant and the member complained against are in very different positions and have different needs. A therapist who is being complained against, is professionally vulnerable and in particular need of support. This support includes but is not limited to legal support. The costs of preparing a "defence" for an adjudication can be prohibitive. One person I spoke to, who was exonerated by the adjudication panel, spent upwards of £10,000 on legal assistance with an extremely complicated set of allegations. Clients who complain against their former therapists are able to get support from Witness (formerly POPAN), which includes formulating their written submissions and bringing someone with them to the hearing who is experienced in helping people to navigate the proceedings.

The handling of a complaint is a complex process that requires attention to complex psychological issues, particularly transference dynamics and cultural issues involving power, race, gender, sexuality and the ability to assimilate information. Addressing these issues in the screening process does not negate the possibility that the complainant has a genuine grievance. Enforcing a policy that includes mediation as a first step in complaints that do not allege serious malpractice would, I believe, contain and diffuse these dynamics so that the heart of the matter can be addressed and that reparation can be made by a practitioner who is not hampered by the fear of humiliation, punishment and further reprisals.

In the course of my research for this book I discovered that the United Kingdom Association of Humanistic Psychology Practitioners (ukAHPP) who accredits psychotherapists through the HIPS (Humanistic and Integrative Psychotherapy Section) of the UKCP had such a procedure in place. In the next chapter, Bee Springwood, who was instrumental in devising the procedure, shows how it can be and is used effectively.

NOTE

1. I must say that I struggle with the principle of autonomy as I have seen it used by investigating panels to mean that the client has the right to do whatever she feels is right, even if it means bringing the therapy to a premature ending, particularly when there is a contract between client and therapist to "hang in there" when things get difficult, as was the case with Teresa and Tamara.

CHAPTER SEVEN

The courage to be human: a humanistic approach to conflict resolution

Bee Springwood

These are my personal reflections on my experience of being both a practitioner and an ethics officer of a small accrediting organisation with humanistic principles at its core.

Throughout my 25 years of practice, I have been lucky not to be subject to a complaint myself. I have done naïve things, careless things, and probably failed to do or to notice other things that were important to my clients. I am also aware of the things I have done—and agonised about afterwards—that led to learning for me and a deepening of the therapeutic relationship. It is not special wisdom or particular caution that has saved me, though I have learned lots over my ten years at the ethical coalface. It is more likely that I have learned a proper humility, which I am grateful to have had modelled for me by some of my supervisors and trainers. To me, the word "humanistic" before "psychotherapy" means accepting that we are never perfect; that in sharing our humanity with clients we must also acknowledge our mistakes and show a willingness to work through any disagreements. In my experience, not only is this the best course of action for protecting myself and my clients from the kinds of complaints that result from a bad or unplanned ending, but it is usually the most therapeutically fruitful.

It is the essence of humanistic practice to negotiate subtle bound-aries, to gradually become wholly human in a "real" relationship. This means we run the risk when showing our humanity in the ther-apeutic relationship of being seen and, in being seen, being misinter-preted, and potentially abused by clients. Both the client and the therapist need to take risks in order for the therapy to be effective. And, in my experience, "mistakes" in therapy are often gifts, that when accepted by both parties to the encounter can move the work forward. This can make it all the more painful when, once a client expresses her displeasure with the therapist or the therapy, our accrediting organisations, (and behind them the phantom stalking the arena which is statutory regulated practice) seem to panic and escape into "legalism", putting a practitioner in the place of defend-ing her actions, rather than to be able to learn from them.

As a small organisation we have had comparatively few com-plaints to deal with over the last ten years. This has given us the lux-ury of time to think about alternative processes for handling com-plaints that larger organisations may not have. Having said that, I have also been asked to mediate in external disputes, and to sit on formal adjudication panels for other organisations. This has given me an outsider's perspective and confirmed my suspicions that, however well managed, formal procedures borrow their energetic quality from legal frameworks, where winning and losing replace a sense of natural justice. Blame is apportioned in place of responsibil-ity; the desire for vengeance and accountability overshadows any possibility of resolution. I have also been part of the team in the ukAHPP (United Kingdom Association of Humanistic Psychology Practitioners) that has designed and piloted a mediation process for complaints, which in the six years that it has been operating, has proved both manageable for the organisation and satisfactory to all the participants. Having said that, I want to emphasise that the views I express here are from my personal experience of being involved in the management and process of complaints for several organisations and are not specific to any one.

Types of complaints and the ground from where they arise

Overall, the need to acknowledge difficulties as an inevitable part of the life of therapy, rather than something to be eradicated by ethical codes and/or legislation, feels very human, and all too humanly complex. As I see it, the difficulties between therapist and client that result in a complaint exist on a continuum of difficulties. These difficulties can arise from a lack of fit between the personalities or the philosophies of each participant in a relationship or from difficulties with content or approach. Figure 1, below, is my attempt to map the continuum of attitudes or behaviours that both client and therapist can take up, in or outside of the therapeutic relationship. These attitudes, when enacted by the client, are usually outside of her awareness. A therapist's supervision will, ideally, help her to get a bird's eye view of the continuum and to manage her obvious reactions to the client's behaviours as well as what may be out of her own awareness. The client may not have such "impartial" support in viewing the therapeutic relationship and may become fixed at one point of the continuum. So will the therapist who has "blind-spots" or who does not take her professional support seriously.

Stalking or Predatory attitude	Hostile or Hyper-critical	Engaged in relationship despite transference issues of dependence/conflict	Helpless or 'victim' attitude	Functionally regressed
Blameless or Naïve	Unthinking or Careless	Engaged in relationship whilst supportive and challenging Attends to own process in supervision/therapy	Self-serving/ Rescuing/ Controlling	Abusive / Negligent

As you can see when both client and therapist are working in the centre of the continua the "real" relationship and the transference issues that it evokes are supported by a working alliance and by the therapist's professional support in supervision or therapy. It is easy to see, though, how a naïve, well-meaning but inexperienced therapist may be impacted by a client who is hostile or hyper-critical or who sees herself as a victim.

In any relationship—and the therapeutic relationship is no exception—the personality issues of one party may activate the more problematic personality issues of the other that may otherwise lie dormant or be kept under control. The power dynamics of the therapeutic relationship may activate more child-like parts of an otherwise high-functioning client which may then invite more parental (rescuing or punishing) or equally childlike (competitive or manipulating) parts of the therapist. Again, ideally, what is activated in the therapist is picked up in supervision or therapy but it is always possible for the therapist to hide some personality traits from the supervisor. Furthermore some humanistic trainings do not emphasise attending to aspects of the therapeutic frame (see Chapter 2) nor do they equip the therapist with the assessment skills that are essential to effective practice. The diagram below illustrates how the personality issues of both client and therapist, including the therapist's training "gaps" or deficits, can lead to ruptures in the therapeutic relationship. When these issues are in conflict, or are out of the therapist's awareness both client and therapist are vulnerable to abuse or to being abused.

The image that seems to prey on the minds of regulating bodies like the UKCP and BACP and is portrayed in the popular press is of the deliberately abusive therapist preying on unsuspecting clients, who are often portrayed as innocent victims rather than capable adults. This scenario is indicated at the far right end of figure 2 and is at the extreme end of the scale. I have come to experience the dynamics on the other end of the scale all too frequently of late where a client with a history of childhood abuse becomes the predator or abuser and the therapist is forced into having to defend herself against the client's actions.

Abused or invaded as a child and seeks revenge/justice	Projects "control" or authority on to other and is hostile/withdrawn	Splits therapist into "good" and "bad" and acts out	Able to hold and express feelings of love, hate, terror, loss	Does not easily feel "seen" or "met". Lacks empathy	Expects not to be heard. Passive expressions of dissatisfaction

Client's personality issues

Therapist's personality issues or training gaps

Over concerned for others. Rescuing. Impotent.	Reactive and careless. Responds without thinking. Not aware of transferential issues	Mismanages boundaries or contracts	Able to be "real" *and* therapeutically effective.	Misuses charisma. Manipulates or invites admiration/ dependence. Lacks empathy.	Is sadistic or deliberately abusive

Increasingly therapists that I meet are becoming concerned about being forced to work in a manner that stifles their spontaneity and creativity in order to protect themselves from what seems like the inevitability of accusations from their client that could seriously affect their personal life and professional standing (see Chapter 6). I have heard of more than one instance where a therapist has felt stalked by a former client and fears for his physical safety and the safety of his family and property.

My experience as a practitioner and ethics officer is that the most common difficulties between client and therapist that may end up in a complaint arise from ruptures in the working alliance, intrusions into the therapeutic frame, unwitting mistakes in managing the transference, the clumsiness that might come from inexperience or the carelessness that can come from stress and fatigue.

These issues all cluster in the mid section of the both diagrams where "good enough" therapy usually succeeds despite–or even because of–mistakes or misattunements. This mid section is not about abuse, but about the muddles in the middle. These are the kinds of boundary disturbances that are discussed in Chapter 2.

Some personal reflections

As therapists we cannot legislate for or demand that our clients be available for change, but we can at least know ourselves and our vulnerabilities better. This is why I believe a trainee psychotherapist's own psychotherapy is so vital to the profession's future survival and ethical safety. Not only do we live through the real, experiential, power shift of being in the other chair, but there is an opportunity to see mirrored in our training therapist, some of the habits of relating which we are likely to take on in our future practice, and where they might lead. I was unlucky to have done my original training in the 70s, when individual work was not deemed essential. I learned a lot from observing and experiencing how the trainers worked in the group when I was a trainee, but did not learn that what might be helpful and facilitative interventions in a group might not translate to being helpful and facilitative in a more intimate and private one-to-one situation. I have found that the emphasis that many humanistic trainings place on working predominately in the group can lead well-meaning, newly qualified therapists into ethical hot water when they get into working individually with clients.

When I finally did go into individual therapy after six years of practice, I did some important personal work in recognising how my world view lay at the naïve end of the spectrum (see fig. 1). I recall my therapist pointing out, gently but firmly, that there are people in the world who *do* intend to do harm, and possibly, even, to me! I learned that in both my personal and professional life, I should not always look to myself to adapt *and* change to make others comfortable. My own best interest took on a new meaning and value when given more equal weight to my client's best interest.

If we look again at the continua of attitudes and behaviours of both the client and the therapist (see fig. 2), we can see how any combination of attitudes and behaviours can create conflict that might damage or lay bare the absence of a functioning working alliance. Once this failure of the alliance is exposed, we might have the courage to seek facilitation as a back up, or we may run and hide in our habits, which we are likely to do under pressure and out of fear and shame. These are the sort of conflicts that are likely to end up as formal complaints.

We are practicing as humanistic therapists in the age of the "blame culture" and the of educated consumer. In the face of this there is a sort of default panic that may engage the therapist who makes a mistake and/or is complained against. As such a therapist, especially if I feel unsupported by my accrediting organisation, I might feel desperate to restore or retain my good name, even resorting to legal support where there is none officially available from the professional organisation. This is an understandable defensiveness. Sometimes, supervisors can get caught up in the defending position too, because, to some extent, their work is being called into question. They may have much professionally and personally invested in championing their supervisee.

Having a complaint taken out by a former client can shake our core understanding of our values and "methods". The colleagues who we dare to tell about the complaint can appear to be supportive in person but may silently be making snap judgements about our innocence or guilt. As is typical of "tribal" shame reactions, we are quick to protect or to shun, in order to protect ourselves. I have known of an example where, when a therapist reached out to other therapists in his immediate community for support, the others withdrew out of some kind of fear of contamination or guilt by association. To make the therapist feel more unsafe, the supervisor was also taken ill and decided to retire early, compounding the feeling of rejection by the peer community. The complaint was not upheld.

As an aggrieved client, in my angry-often vengeful-state I may want to do some permanent damage. Fantasies of regaining some power, being able to put the therapist out of work, or of openly naming and shaming her, might take over from staying with my feelings of hurt or disappointment. What usually goes missing is any idea that there might be some value in what may be occurring; to see that it could be an opportunity to restore, or make a new, working alliance, one in which the work of therapy can be reassessed, and some value retained, whilst "mistakes" can be placed in the context of ordinary human failing.

For any healing or resolution to occur in this climate of fear and retribution there needs to be an openness, which in turn has to be facilitated by others outside the original dyad, who can step in to help with the repair and review of the work. There is, as with all models of restorative justice, a place for natural justice to emerge from the theatre of fear, revenge and indignation. This needs to happen in a sort of "play space" where serious work can occur, but in which the threat of outcomes is put at a temporary distance.

Some such sense of natural justice for one party, or both, may occur in the eventual outcome of a formal complaint, but its likely to be in spite, rather than because, of the formality. Examples from other fields, even ones where professional competences can be clearly defined and taught, do not serve us well as helpful models. We see in the papers countless libel cases, where blame has to be apportioned on one side only, and settlements fly in the face of rational recompense. Fear of legal consequences reduces caring professionals to the caricature of dodgy car salesmen mincing their words to avoid the truth.

Although many of the examples discussed in Chapter 2 derive from naïve practitioners, interestingly we have discovered that inexperienced practitioners may be less vulnerable to being complained against. The "new therapist on the block" may, in fact, be quicker to apologise than a more experienced colleague, even admitting her own inexperience and owning it as part of the problem. Experience seems to bring about the need to justify our interventions with theory and more theory rather than to explore them with an attitude of curiosity and in a context of co-creation. Is it possible, in my growing complacency over the years, that I have become so used to my own quirks that I may not notice when I am missing or failing or just

over-riding a client by pulling rank? The need to bring one's everyday work to supervision is the crucial thing here.

In my own experience of working with clients who have brought
complaints against members of the medical profession, the issue
that remained with them long after formal resolution was mostly the
fruitless wait for someone to say sorry for the unintended anguish
caused. The hurt that is experienced by both parties when one psyche rubs up against another is not so easily remedied by an insurance settlement.

I have been reminded more than once in administering complaints of the comparison with the etiquette about car accidents. I
have heard people saying one should not apologise on the roadside,
because it admits liability. I'm glad I have not had to put this to the
test recently in my clinical practice and wonder if, in the current climate, we are being encouraged to be wary of apologising, if we
believe we have inadvertently caused harm.

It is also a real concern for therapists that we could have our
practice destroyed by a former client who is acting out an
un-worked-through negative transference. Many of my colleagues
believe that the therapeutic contract extends even when the therapy
has broken down and say they would not defend themselves against
a client who has left parts of herself with the therapist, even if that
client is attacking them. These situations are made much worse for
the therapist when the professional organisation seems to be gang-
ing up on them, threatening suspensions, expulsions and exposure
in professional journals.

One of my concerns about statutory accreditation for psychotherapy and counselling is that we will become hand tied in a similar
way. Since therapy is an art of attunement, and not a measurable skill
like surgery or car mechanics, will organisations like the ukAHPP be
free to respond within a humanistic framework when things, as they
inevitably do at times, go wrong between two basically well-intentioned people, one of whom is seeking help from the other?

A humanistic approach to conflict resolution

Between 1998 and 2000, ukAHPP developed a structured system of
mediation as a more holistic means of dealing with complaints. This
involved some training for therapy practitioners to explore the

process, and understand the need for an approach which was more likely to ensure effective outcomes, compared to the atmosphere of frustration, blame, distrust, disappointment, revenge, fear, and, not least, the administrative and emotional exhaustion that had surrounded so many of our complaints procedures.

We developed a statement of the philosophy of mediation, of why there needs to be an alternative to the "old" way of addressing both formal complaints and also the smaller but painful difficulties that may arise between therapist and client. The organisation already had a system of facilitation for both sides of a complaint that swung into action as soon as a complaint was made, which we were able to incorporate into the new mediation-centred procedure.

I took on the position of chair of the Ethics Committee to steer the organisation through this next phase, specifically because this process connected me back to my roots in humanistic values in the late seventies. Back then, I was involved quite a bit with exploring "co-operative dynamics" in small groups and communities, and became interested in conflict resolution as part of group experience.

The kinds of concerns that were echoed by other Ethics Committee members, drawing us together in a common interest to address what we and colleagues saw as the sticky end of the accredited therapy world, were various. Each of us had experiences of therapeutic ruptures, either from our own, or our colleagues' bad experiences or lucky escapes. We shared a sense that our and others' original training had been poor in the areas of ethical thinking and practice. We were concerned about the lack of any structure for post-qualifying support in dealing with difficulties and breaks in contact within the therapeutic relationship through the lens of the humanistic philosophy that we all shared.

As more "senior" members of a humanistic organisation that accredits psychotherapists to register with the UKCP we were committed to the notion that conflict can be resolved, and that mediation was the process best modelling the humanistic principles that call for the inclusion of *all* the dimensions of an experience. We were agreed that we needed a procedure for conflict resolution that would include facts, thoughts, feelings, body process and the witnessing of these by others.

Written procedures and codes are important guidelines for us in maintaining good, ethical practice. But rulebooks cannot in themselves address the emotional and spiritual needs of both parties to a dispute—who are equally human beings—that have to be faced if either party is to feel fully acknowledged and arrive at sense of resolution.

We began to explore the question, "What is it we need in order to *feel* resolved?" We wanted to explore in more sensory detail the territory or culture from which most complaints arise in order to explore the flavour as opposed to the statistics of the arena of complaints against or about psychotherapists. The point is not always that someone has actually broken any written codes, but that the client just *feels* hurt or damaged or hard done by. Much of this discrepancy might be attributed to the mismatch of style of each party (see fig. 1). As an organisation we had experience of seeing that this was where facilitation came into its own, helping both parties to a complaint to focus on the lost but reclaimable outcomes, providing the missing observer position that so often leaves the room when two people get entrenched in their positions.

We had also seen that facilitation to both parties to a complaint worked less well towards supporting resolution when a real working alliance had failed to be achieved in the therapy. If either client or therapist has fixed personality traits that are not accessible to self-reflection or change and if the therapy has broken down *because* this willingness to change is fundamentally missing on either side, a facilitator to one party only can not conjure it up.

Ideally a complaints procedure based on humanistic principles needs to address the injury and at the same time encourage both parties to a complaint to accept each other's humanity, warts and all, whilst striving for and supporting excellence in practice.

As an organisation of and for humanistic practitioners, we fully support the hearing of all sides of a conflict, to allow room and support for each party to acknowledge their mistakes or contributions without resorting to blaming and scapegoating. The need to address feelings of regret, loss, anger, disappointment is most readily met by a system which has the many human faces of mediation readily available. It is the most direct means for a complainant to challenge bad practice and gain redress, and it is the best-known form in many situations of de-escalating conflict.

I will share with you here the process currently being operated by the ukAHPP and hope to encourage dialogue within your

professional communities and organisations that may lead to some
of these principles being taken forward into the wider community.

The mediation process—a map

In the current climate of "rule-based" ethics we needed to be clear
about when and how mediation would constitute a suitable course
of action in a formal ethical complaint?

Provided the grounds for a complaint do not appear *prima facie*
to be such a serious breach of conduct that a meeting would be likely to intimidate the complainant or the member complained against,
then mediation as a face-to-face process is actively encouraged, to
co-create a resolution. A too-serious breach would be evident sexual
abuse, violence, or financial threats and intimidation, where the person complaining does not feel, even with substantial support, that
they can be safe in the same space. Sometimes this takes time to
decide. But even in those cases where one party refuses to meet the
other we carry out the process of mediation at a distance. This is
cumbersome but has proved to be ultimately effective.

The role of the facilitator is of primary importance throughout
all ukAHPP disputes or complaints. This is a psychotherapist who,
having prior experience or support from the ethics team, volunteers
to provide support to someone who is in the process of making a
complaint to help them decide what they are hoping to achieve and
what course of action they want to take. Very often, the process of
being heard-fully—by a third party who conveys impartiality and
lack of interest in the outcome can, of itself, provide the solution.
When this does not happen and the complainant believes that there
are grounds for making a formal complaint, she is usually able to
feel supported enough by the process of facilitation to face the
therapist, (or supervisor, or trainer) and to enter into a process of
dialogue and mediation. We have found that these face-to-face
meetings are an important part of the healing process. The complainant who feels empowered by the facilitation process and held
by the procedures that require mediation as the first step in any formal procedure can meet the therapist on what feels like more equal
ground. In the mind of the person who feels hurt or abused there is
a restoration of power, of a sense of fairness. The "perpetrator" has
to sit in a situation where he is no longer in control. For the person

who feels "wronged" just to meet the therapist on more equal ground, where each feels vulnerable and is also receiving support, can provide a sense of completion without the need to become adversarial.

At the first mention that someone is considering making or has made a complaint against one of our members a facilitator is appointed for the complainant. This is someone who knows the ropes of our organisation, and has access to the Ethics Committee for consultation. As a voluntary organisation, we rely on our members who have experience or have used our training in mediation, to put themselves forward to participate in this process. Even practitioners who do not have formal training in mediation find they have the skills to act as facilitators. Reflective listening, holding boundaries around safety, framing suggestions as options and not orders, checking that both parties are feeling heard are skills possessed by anyone with experience of working with couples or groups.

The main difference between couples or group work and mediation is focus. Mediation between an aggrieved client and an anxious therapist needs to retain a focus on moving forward, either together or individually. With the knowledge that the parties may only meet for one session comes the need to be more focussed on options and decision making by naming the choices facing each participant without being directive. These choices include apologising, agreeing to seek more supervision or training, resuming the therapy, agreeing to disagree, or moving on to a formal hearing. The only goal of the mediation process is to gain the agreement of both parties to move forward in a way that is mutually accepted.

To say that mediation is informal is not the same as to say it is casual. All participants, including the Ethics Committee who oversee the process, need to be scrupulous about the methodology. For both parties, a complaint is a serious matter and feelings, which run high, need respectful and compassionate containment.

Stage 1

When the Ethics Committee receives notification that someone wants to or is thinking about taking out a complaint a co-ordinator, nearly always from within the Ethics Committee, is appointed who then appoints a facilitator for the complainant.

There follows an active exploration by the facilitator with the complainant of the nature of the complaint; of which, if any, codes have been broken as well as of the complainant's subjective experience. The focus at this stage is on the needs and wants of the complainant. Focussing on the complainant's subjective experience is a subtle process of helping her to understand more about her expectations of the therapist and the organisation. What are the expectations of redress and/or punishment? What are the fantasies and fears around being heard by the facilitator who, after all, represents the organisation in the complainant's mind and may even be seen as protecting the therapist. (In our organisation we judge that even if no codes have been broken there may be a breakdown of sufficient gravity for the client to be supported to meet with their therapist. In this instance both parties take part in a mediation process without the possibility of formal sanctions).

If codes have been broken, then the facilitator helps the client consider what might be the likely outcome of a formal hearing including helping her to see that, even if sanctions are imposed in a quasi-judicial procedure, she may not at all feel like she has won as these processes are so often acted out on an attack/defend continuum. It is important at this stage for the client to develop a realistic awareness of the possible outcomes, including the awareness that the confidentiality that was promised by the therapist may be broken, to the further detriment of the client, in order for the therapist to defend himself.

In most cases, the knowledge that mediation is a real option may bring instant relief to the complainant. In others, helping the complainant to reach the point where she is open to the mediation process takes much longer. For the facilitator this means walking a careful line of listening and supporting on the one hand and not restarting "therapy" on the other. To do so would be to fall into the trap of taking over where the "failed" therapist left off and would only serve to transfer or to compound the problem.

Stage 2

Once mediation is agreed and the complaint has taken some "shape" in the mind of the complainant, the facilitator informs the co-ordinator who only then informs the therapist about the complaint. At that time the co-ordinator appoints a facilitator for the therapist. In some cases this is a colleague who is suggested by the therapist as someone she respects but does not know well.

The therapist is not free to refuse face-to-face mediation except on the same grounds as the client, out of fear of intimidation and threat. But even in cases where no physical threat exists, the therapist may feel that her very sense of her own configuration of herself as a competent and ethical practitioner is under threat. Facilitation for the therapist from the moment she is told of a complaint being made against her helps to shift the desire to hide in shame on the one hand and to defend by attacking on the other. We have found that therapists who do not receive support from a designated colleague are likely to become vulnerable to poor judgement or to overcompensation. There is a human tendency when feeling attacked to react by pathologising the client or to become so safety conscious that therapy with other clients ceases to be effective. Some therapists have even stopped working altogether.

The facilitator needs to help the therapist explore the "case to answer", and to formulate a response to the written complaint, integrating the therapist's subjective experience and theoretical understanding. The therapist may need help to get to a more simple level of human connection with the complainant, and to see what things may be possible to acknowledge or offer to this client in mediation. The facilitator can help the therapist to see that it will be important not to react with a need to outwit the client with interpretations of the transference, how ever tempting it may be to do so, as to respond in such a way would only serve to continue a failed process outside the "container" of the therapy.

Stage 3

The co-ordinator then appoints a mediator as swiftly as possible from the membership, based on lack of involvement with either party through training or collegial connections and availability. The co-ordinator and the mediator together arrange all the practicalities of time, place and frequency in order to reduce the possibility of manipulative behaviour from any party at this stage. Experience has led us to expect to resolve most disputes with one or two face to face meetings of the parties involved and their respective facilitators and with the mediator on "neutral" territory, in other words not in the therapist's consulting room or any party's home. The organisation funds the cost of hiring a venue for these meetings if it is necessary to do so.

The co-ordinator takes responsibility for managing the transfer of necessary information–any notes, correspondence, reports, tape recordings—for the mediator. All parties to the mediation will have access to this material before the first meeting so that everyone feels equally informed. We are aiming at transparency at this stage.

At the meeting

1. The mediator gives time for both complainant and therapist to be heard, allowing for comments of clarification and support from the facilitators, without interruption or contradiction by either the complainant or the member complained against. The mediator begins the session by reiterating the philosophy of the process which is that, as an organisation founded on humanistic principles, we anticipate that thoughts, feelings, bodily respons-es, spiritual beliefs of both parties will be given equal weight and recognition and that all parties to be treated and *will treat each other* with respect and integrity.

2. Time for each party to respond to this round is then given, also in a structured way. There are echoes of the *pow wow* in this. There is a chance to respond, but not in a reactive way, with time to absorb what has been said before responding built in to the process.

3. Then there is time for both parties to clarify and put forward their wishes for a way forward. For example the therapist who has experienced being "stalked" by her former client may want an agreement that the therapy has ended and that there will be no further contact. The client may want an apology from the therapist or to have the therapist return or destroy notes or tapes of their sessions. Sometimes both parties want to find a way to acknowledge that, in spite of seemingly irresolvable differences of opinion or agreement about the nature of past events, there was no malice intended. When this has been the case both par-ties can be supported to find a creative or symbolic way to end their relationship or to move forward together.

4. If no agreement can be reached at this stage, for reasons that both the mediator and facilitators see as part of a reasonable process, then a future meeting will be arranged, with some "action" to be undertaken by both parties between meetings to be agreed. It is important to have *some* agreement about "next steps" in order for the process not to become a protracted wrangle, in which the failed therapy is somehow re-enacted. There needs to be *something* to do, even if it is simply to go away and think about the options that have been put on the table and those that have not. To leave a meeting with nothing resolved and no plans for moving forward can be very demoralising for the client, a nd professional torture for the therapist.

In the event of the process of mediation breaking down at this stage, the facilitator will then go back to consider again with the complainant the way forward and the desired as well as likely outcome of a formal hearing. This may lead to a revival of the mediation process or to the formal complaints procedure being invoked. This has not happened yet as we have found that disputes between client and therapist have been resolved within the sometimes-arduous process of mediation. The implications, though, are important to consider. If the process of facilitation and mediation has failed to help the parties to find a place of meeting, then, from the client's point of view, will a formal procedure be any better at persuading the therapist of the "wrongs" she has committed? If the client refuses to see that the therapist's actions, however hurtful or unhelpful, came from a place that was naïve or uninformed but did not carry the *intention* to harm, will putting her case in a more formal setting where the therapist appears to be or at least feels on trial bring any closure, even if sanctions are imposed? Recent civil actions against therapists who have been exonerated by formal hearings as well as against those who have been sanctioned might suggest that they are not being effective in achieving resolution.

5. If agreement between both parties has been reached the mediator puts in writing the nature of that agreement and any further action to be taken by either party. A time-scale, if appropriate, is put forward and copies are sent to the parties to the mediation

via the facilitators. The agreement is signed by each party and facilitator and returned to the co-ordinator.

6. It is important that all parties adhere to the time scale agreed. The Co-ordinator needs to be informed of this, and will pursue either party if there are defaults. Again, having had no "live" examples of breakdown at this stage to test, I can only speculate about the implications of what would happen if the agreements that rose out of the mediation process were not kept. This would signal some failure at the mediation stage and it might be that the organisation would need to resort to the formal complaints procedure. My sense is that a second "mediation phase" might be fruitful, as I know it can be in neighbourhood disputes. It might be that something has been missed in the original agreement and that it needs to be adjusted or re-written.

No creativity is without struggle

I cannot begin to describe the charged atmosphere and vivid "to and fro" of a mediation process. Each person present is, on the one hand, following a formula, a set of clear guidelines that is, on the other hand, unique to each case and each configuration of personalities and histories. Just like a therapy session. Suffice it to say that, when I have been involved, there has always been an experience of sitting with the painfulness of impasse, the struggle to be understood. Sometimes there is a feeling of going to the brink of frustration and fear of the conflict being revived, or exacerbated. But when it works–and it does work—there is tremendous relief and even elation at the experiencing of human beings having such painful disagreements and still breaking through to resolution. Often that resolution has proved creative in itself, and provided a way forward for one or both parties. Of course, like many creative products, we would not have chosen to get there down such a rocky path, and to devote such time and trouble. But creativity often takes us on longer and more varied journeys than we first or ever expected. How much that is beautiful would never have been made if its maker or makers had known what the real costs would be. Is this not also true of successful psychotherapy itself?

CHAPTER EIGHT

"Everything's fine here"–or is it? A mirror on our training institutions

Sue Jones

In psychotherapy training we often talk about mirroring and reflecting. The person centred approach mirrors back the experience of the client through empathic understanding of her frame of reference, the psychoanalytic approach holds up a mirror to the revealing world of projections. Just before his death Ian Gordon Brown held up a mirror, not to us as clients or practitioners, but as trainers and training institutions. He challenged us to see a shadow in the carefully polished glass, suggesting that in "caring" institutions it is the issue of power struggle that is denied. Speaking about the pressures associated with power in organisations he wrote:

> *On the one hand, in groups based on the ethos and attitude of love, those concerned with caring, the power struggle is terrific, and it's always unconscious. On the other hand, in industrial organisations, where the power struggles are overt, everybody knows who is on a power trip, people joke about it, pull the other person's leg, it's all open and above board and it's something else that is unconscious. Jung talked about the polarity not of love and hate so much as love and power. Where there is power, love can't exist and vice-versa. People in the first kind of organisation where the love aspect is conscious, would flatly deny that there is any power struggle at all.... [Gordon Brown, 2002, p. 152]*

The title for this chapter is an attempt to capture my own experience of visiting a number of organisations and institutions in the course of carrying out research into their "health" as seen through their experience of and management of complaints. Almost without exception I was initially encouraged by the management to believe that "Everything's fine here". It was only after digging deeper that I began to see this attitude on the part of management as an apparently necessary myth, unconsciously constructed to hold the system together. The impression I was given seemed to jar with the reality of life's ups and downs, and indeed my previous subjective experience of organisational dynamics.

I began to focus on organisational dynamics when I headed a new counselling and psychotherapy training school in East Anglia. I had already been a trainer in several organisations and had witnessed first hand the enormous distress that can occur when things go wrong. This took me back to my own need to please authority, and how as a student I suffered quietly and co-operated compliantly with those I trusted to be in charge of my training and future career. Making a complaint would not have been an option out of fear of being seen as a "bad" therapist. I have found since that I am not alone in having had these experiences.

As we started building the foundation of our new training organisation, colleagues and I grappled with the ground blocks, to ensure, as far as we were able, that the ethos, structure and procedures would be those that we wanted to and could live by. Our hearts were in the process and it was serious business. We were driven by passion and an energetic desire to create something new and congruent with our beliefs. But how, we wondered, could we avoid the problems we had not only witnessed but had inadvertently been entangled in, if they were in a sense invisible—implicit rather than explicit?

I needed to understand more about institutions and complaints procedures in order to bring into awareness what I and others knew existed but were unable to pinpoint and to articulate explicitly. Questions led to more questions and this eventually evolved into an action research project. My aim was to explore the effects of complaints procedures on individuals within organisations by gathering and analysing themes from focus groups. The results from this project reinforced my view that complaints procedures, as they commonly stood, were only the tip of the iceberg. It was as if the boats that floated on top of the surface were hinting at, but not revealing, what was lurking beneath.

The data that I gathered through interviewing trainers, trainees and management, showed conclusively that complaints processes were imagined to be frightening and traumatising. Interestingly, although Palmer Barnes (1998) writes that training matters form the basis of roughly one third of all formal complaints to the UKCP, my experience of interviewing members of training organisations showed a collective belief that complaining led, not to better organisational and training practices, but to the complainant being sidelined or outcast. My own experience is that students in training rarely make formal complaints. This left me wondering: if students do not complain whilst in training are we sitting too comfortably and what are we missing in the development of our training institutions?

In doing this research I have been on my own journey of development. I do not profess to have the answers or to be a paragon of virtue! I also do not want to blame or shine a light on anyone's particular failings or difficulties. Leadership in a training organisation is a highly complex process and through my own experience I have been forced to open my eyes to personal traits that I might otherwise have avoided looking at. I have frequently been brought very uncomfortably face to face with my own inadequacies and lack of foresight. I have had to look more closely at the concept of shadow (Jung, 1938) and my own blind spots. For me, having others around me as a mirror and making time to reflect—on my own, and with colleagues and students—is an ongoing, enlivening and occasionally painful journey of self-discovery.

Dare we look at the shadow in our training institutions? Exploring the shadow side of anything is a difficult exercise as by definition the shadow is unspoken, unacknowledged and denied. By its very nature it is "unknowable". What follow are composites taken from many interviews with trainers and staff in psychotherapy training institutions, and from my own experience as former trainee and trainer, and now as a director of a training institute. The vignettes described in this chapter are all composites taken from data collected for research purposes, and not to be attributed to any one person or organisation. I want to suggest that these are areas for managers, trainers and accrediting bodies to seriously consider as a conceptual framework for re-formulating institutional complaint procedures.

Although good psychotherapy practice must be supported by a knowledge of the limits of intimacy and connectedness, a large proportion of the stories I heard on my travels included ones of sexual breaches and muddled boundaries. All of these were whispered in coded communication, making it difficult to discuss these things openly. Transferential phenomena within organisations are inevitable and have been well documented (Diamond, 1993). Kearns (2005) has written of the "transferential web" that impacts all involved in the "field" (Lewin, 1952) of psychotherapy training. She explores the paradox that most of the relational issues addressed in the training are the very ones that the majority of trainees are struggling with for the first time. The students are hungry for learning but they are being encouraged to look inwards for that learning. Many of these students are also hungry for healing. They look to their tutors, supervisors and therapists to model "healthy" relational contact where their families of origin did not. Diamond writes that these hierarchical interactions are often filled with re-enactments of the dependency, attachment, separation, and individuation dilemmas of parent-infant relationships. It seems hardly surprising that things go wrong with boundaries being breached and people ending up hurt and disillusioned. Some accrediting bodies require ongoing personal therapy for students while in training, but in 2005 the British Association for Counselling and Psychotherapy dropped this requirement. In my view this is likely to mean that students who are not in their own therapy will look more to the trainers for support. They will also not have a forum in which to process some of the transference issues that emerge in the training group or in the organisation as a whole. How, I wonder, will the trainers be able to cope with this?

I have identified below what I believe to be three areas within psychotherapy institutes that are particularly problematic. These are areas that naturally exist in all types of organisations but I believe, from both personal experience and my research data, that they present particular challenges in psychotherapy and counselling organisations. The areas overlap and interconnect. Out of these I have drawn three core themes that I believe we need to seriously consider as areas for exploration and improvement. I will explore those themes and then go on to offer my own suggestions as to how to move forward. I believe that the interplay between these areas is not only poorly understood but creates an environment in which individuals may suffer and silently tolerate abuse, without understanding or having the power to complain for fear of reprisal. The organisation has the key to career success and the individual–trainee or trainer— does not want to risk that being taken away or withheld. It is as if a complaint could make an individual unworthy or unfit to become a full member of the club.

Cult-ure

I believe that we are at an embryonic stage in our understanding of how to train psychotherapists and counsellors and to manage our training institutions. The literature and my data reinforced my thinking that we need to attend to the hidden, more subtle cultural behaviours embedded in these systems in order to provide the foundation from which our future psychotherapists can learn and grow.

Diamond (1993, p. 97) wrote about the unconscious life of organisations and the inherent instability of work groups, expanding on the theme by using a psychodynamic developmental framework. Diamond suggests that the unconscious actions and covert goals in a work group correspond to the degree of development of the leader. The earlier the wound of the leader the more primitive and regressed the group is, in order to defend against the anxiety of identity annihilation. Kernberg (1998, p. 204) later wrote about institutional problems in psychoanalytic education highlighting the unconscious regression and transferential dynamics that get re-enacted.

Sally, a conscientious and diligent trainee psychotherapist, left a group in tears during a training session. Sally was an incest survivor and the subject for the training day was shame. The trainer, also the programme leader, followed her into the garden, leaving the group to continue on their own. He sat down on the grass beside her. Sitting himself close to her he put his arm around her shoulders and comforted her. She wept.

"I'm really sorry I left the room, I feel so bad"

The trainer then began to stroke Sally's thigh.

"You are such an attractive and beautiful woman when you cry"

Sally froze. Her history had always been a secret for her and she was just beginning to work through this in her own therapy. She could not tell the trainer to stop nor could she possibly complain. If she resisted his attention would he punish her by giving her dissertation a bad mark? Would he say she would not make a psychotherapist, or worse still—could he throw her off the course? Sally now had a new secret to keep. They returned to the group and carried on with the teaching session.

In his paper on cult characteristics and psychotherapy institutions Robertson warns us of the implicit learning that occurs and the impact it has on emerging therapists in dysfunctional training systems. He lists eight potentially destructive characteristics found in psychotherapy institutions (Robertson, 1993). Although initially shocked by his characterisations I found each of Robertson's cult characteristics to be embedded in my research data.

- A closed system
- Group conformity
- Idealisation of the leader
- Scapegoating
- Charismatic vision
- Denial of shadow
- Group narcissism
- Secrets

I found that what had begun as a passionate, personal vision frequently took on a transpersonal edge that became narcissistic in quality. People who resisted it seemed to be sidelined, eventually leaving. I remember one situation where a trainer leading a day's workshop set an assignment to be completed in the morning sessions and didn't turn up until well after lunch. When some of the participants protested, they were told "If you don't like it you can leave". None did.

In gathering my research data I heard many stories of dramas attached to the much-loved charismatic trainer. These included favoured students who passed examinations with a nod and a wink, students in the "inner circle" who were employed and elevated to a particular status despite the reservations of other senior staff. Adoration of the head of the course or institute as "guru" was the norm. I also heard stories of destructive and damaging behaviours on the part of those "gurus"–alcohol and drug abuse, sexual indiscretions, financial impropriety—that could not be challenged by either staff or students. Tentative protesters were seen as saboteurs and often shamed with brutal humiliation in front of peers. More compliant students stayed silent, coming to believe that silence and collusion were the price to be paid for future success.

George had been a senior trainer for many years and was proud of the way he ran his sessions. He was entertaining and exciting and the students loved it. "Don't worry about these hours for the exam board", George told Tony at his one to one tutorial. "I know better than them and one day you'll be teaching here–you're in my inner circle". What wasn't so exciting about George was the way he used barbed comments. "Hey, Elephant Legs" he called out one day to Louise. Louise would not complain. If she ignored it she might be invited to be a tutor too.

I found secrets everywhere. Interestingly the concept of confidentiality both enabled these to be told and enabled them to remain secret. I was told of several situations where the breach of sexual boundaries by a trainer remained a secret as "the student's confidentiality had to be protected". This left me feeling uneasy about how we use our understanding of confidentiality in psychotherapy.

I was surprised to find how few forums in general there were for open dialogue. Where there were staff meetings they were not obligatory, poorly attended or agendas were so packed there was little time for free communication. I found that what was really being felt by individuals was not able to be openly expressed in the system. A tendency to control by pathologising combined with a "be nice" culture drove conflict and any acknowledgement of shadow underground.

I found frequent evidence of narcissistic leaders who required their "followers" to admire them and share their vision. My belief is that this, combined with the closed and incestuous system of recruitment, which seemed to be common practice almost everywhere, leads to lack of regenerative input from the outside world and contributes to a narcissistic culture characterised by closed thinking, a strongly idealised organisational self image and stagnation of ideas. This type of culture seemed to linger even after a leader had left. The organisation was unable to look inwards, and if challenged, pushed all undesirable aspects outside on to a safe target or alternatively scapegoated someone within who could then be pushed out or side-lined, leaving the system intact. The grandiose self-image survived despite the cuckoo having flown the nest.

The history of psychotherapy training, in particular humanistic, is historically relatively short in comparison to the amount of growth. Kearns (2005) has written that she believes humanistic trainings are turning out under-supported psychotherapists whose assessment and diagnostic skills are poor. I would add that I believe that humanistic psychotherapy and counselling trainings are in general at an embryonic stage of development and out of sync with the current climate of business. Despite there being some in-depth literature already on organisational dynamics (Huffington, Armstrong, et al. 2004) I found the difficulties described below seemed to apply to all orientations throughout the psychotherapy field.

As I see it humanistic and integrative psychotherapy is about understanding human behaviour, facilitating growth, safe conflict and change in a respectful environment of non-oppressive practice: all in the service of the client. This is what we profess to do and teach in our training establishments. There is an overarching theory and way of being in the world that connects and holds us. To carry this is an onerous task for trainers who have responsibility for teaching others in an environment where the development of psychotherapy skills and the development of the self are equally weighted with the gaining of theoretical knowledge.

The people who are drawn to work and train in the psychotherapy profession are frequently wounded healers (Sedgwick, 1994). Guggenbuhl-Craig (1968) warns us of the psychotherapist's shadow and its contribution to the misuse of power. He identifies a "healer-patient" archetype (Guggenbuhl-Craig, 1971, p. 85), suggesting that the psychotherapist may be prone to taking on the role of healer/ guru and to leaving the "illness" at the feet of the patient. The shadow of care is neglect and abuse. If we apply this to the teaching arena and couple it with a pupil/teacher transferential relationship of idealisation we can see the possible consequences where an adored, charismatic teacher may project on to and then pathologise the student leaving a trail of disappointment and confusion within the victim.

Mary was a programme leader for the post-graduate diploma and failed to turn up at the college for a training day. A student rang Mary only to find she had forgotten that she was meant to be teaching. The students went home. On their next training day Mary invited them all to her house for an evening's training. Julia could not make that date but when she objected was told that *she* had the problem and should own the fact that she was envious of the attention her peers would receive and that she was acting out her raging inner child. Julia lost a day's training.

I feel sure that it is not difficult for us all to identify with the "lost" feeling when struggling in one's own personal therapy and growing perhaps against the tide of domestic expectations. For students the idealised tutor or training institute may temporarily become the needed idealised "parent". A leader's vision may be inspirational and hold the ideal, thus creating an institutional culture that may have a transpersonal edge. A dangerous combination indeed. The brighter the light, the darker the shadow.

Menzies Lyth (1988) writes of anxiety in the nursing profession. She points us to how the profession arouses strong feelings in the nurse. The defences of detachment and avoidance that are built into the system to defend against that anxiety by the experienced professional nurses, in turn contribute to the stress of the students.

Similarly, psychotherapy institutions are stressful places with inbuilt dynamics and defences that impact on students. The students are struggling with a training that requires the uncovering, understanding and integrating of repressed aspects of themselves. The trainers usually work part-time, and in addition to their regular teaching work, are expected to make extra "voluntary" commitments to the institute while running a private practice or being otherwise employed. Many trainers report being unpaid or badly paid for marking essays and developing the curriculum. They are also expected to attend parties, graduation celebrations and other "social" occasions. Management, particularly course leaders, feel unsupported and isolated yet find that talking to others in similar positions outside the organisation opens up potential fear of competition, failure and shame. Advisory "committees" may well be made up of family members or close friends, thus adding to the leader's collusion in an avoidant or punitive culture hidden beneath a veneer of an idealised mission. In my experience training institutes in general struggle with cultures where caring for others and love of the task are emphasized overtly whilst the shadow of competition, exploitation and ego-boosting goes underground.

Management

The culture of an institute tends to revolve around the leader and his/her vision. Whether we like it or not all groups have leaders. Indeed a group needs a leader to keep the show on the road. Leaders have power and how they use and understand it impacts throughout the whole system.

The leaders within our training establishments are usually psychotherapists who have achieved in their profession and have a vision of how to train others. These leaders often take managerial roles within their systems and my experience is that these different roles are not as clearly defined or understood as they would be in the corporate world. Very often the people at the top of our institutions have little or no managerial training and are juggling part-time teaching with successful private practices. Psychotherapy institutions are expensive to run and an enormous amount of voluntary time and hard work enables them to survive.

Therapists who join institutions to become trainers frequently have clear views built from their own success and autonomy and may not be the natural team players that the system needs. Halpin (2005) describes the personality type of the therapist as being idealistic and capable of great devotion to a person, purpose or cause. I suggest that the same characteristics that work in individual practice are those that contribute to the problems in institutions. These problems may present as the symbiotic relationship between a charismatic leader and devoted other, sexual and other breaches of ethics, unspoken competition around beliefs and attitudes and an independence that gets in the way of open, transparent teamwork in the cohesive running of a business.

Walton (2005) describes leadership as a vital field of study due to the impact upon us all of bad, absent or deluded leadership. The combination of busy people at the top of our institutions, trainers who are used to autonomy and self direction, and students who are looking to their seniors for growth and learning, is like walking a tight rope over a lion's den.

I have gathered many narratives about difficulties with management dynamics. Everyone and every institution had stories to tell about ethical breaches, moral dilemmas, struggles with egos, conflicting views of theory and practice, poor communication, unequal sharing of tasks and money, burn-out, secrets, narcissism, covert abuse and more. I was struck by the generosity of individuals in their sharing of experiences. I also experienced fear and suspicion of me as an outsider, which often led to defensive, carefully monitored speech.

These organisations seemed to have few forums for transparency and free discussion. Management and tutors' meetings were irregular and infrequent and seen as irritating and task-orientated rather than fruitful and enjoyable. Recruitment of trainers was frequently done through asking favoured students, close friends or even lovers. It was the norm for students to finish their training and become in-house trainers–even examiners—themselves.

I believe that these closed systems and incestuous cultures are fertile ground for the shadow. Those who speak out are pathologised and sidelined. Humanistic values are misused by those in positions of power to suppress and confuse issues of competition, envy and neglect. Leaders, who are also at some level fearful of losing much-needed staff, unconsciously collude with the taming and denial of difficult feelings. These organisational cultures impact on the student, who implicitly "learns" about how the "parents" manage our family system: "Do as I say, not as I do".

Having said that, in my research I was struck by the passion and commitment of individual staff members who were prepared to work until they drop at the expense of their own needs. I found this evident in every institution. My sense was that this silenced the dissenting voice leaving him/her implicitly holding the place of the "uninvolved member" of the team. Institutes are often run on a shoestring with the leader working long, usually unpaid, hours. This led to an expectation that others should do the same. Trainers were paid for their teaching time but were expected to do more. This resulted in poor attendance at meetings, envy within the team, fantasies that others are being paid more and many gripes about feeling undervalued.

I discovered that the people at the top were learning as they went along and often had unclear definition of roles. Leaders seemed to muddle psychotherapeutic skills with leadership skills and were often unable to use their authority appropriately. Staff longed for structure yet meetings were filled with facilitation of emotions and process at the expense of task.

Conversely when the figure at the top was generally authoritarian in style this too led to difficulties. Staff felt unable to complain and seemed to give up, taking on a language of complicity and "groupthink" (Janis, 1982). The only alternative was to leave. However there was general consensus that leaving would mean a significant drop in income, not just from teaching, but because students were less likely to seek out a trainer for supervision if she was no longer perceived to be in the inner circle. I was also told of situations where the repressed anger and feelings of powerlessness filtered down to battles within the staff team and, in the worst scenario, in communication with the students. I was told of one trainer who would inappropriately befriend trainees and supervisees and encourage the trainees to act out her own anger. This ended in an affair with a trainee.

Communication

Emotional literacy (Goleman, 1996) is at the heart of psychotherapy. What I found in my interviews was that the ability to express and understand one's own and another's emotional states is a mixed blessing. Like the use of power, it can be consciously or unconsciously misused. At its worst it can be used to attune to another and then to corrupt or control. It may also be used as justification for bad decision making, rationalising one's own behaviours as "feeling right". When clarity is needed emotion can muddy the waters.

More worryingly, theory seemed to be used defensively as an attack against personal threat. I was told of many stories where students felt the trainer had used complex theoretical language in order to avoid a challenge. Students repeatedly recalled that having challenged a trainer, they were responded to with long-winded theory that was multi-levelled and irrelevant. These students recounted finally being told that they were not "robust enough to manage the rigours of psychotherapy training". Students felt shamed and their original questions remained unanswered. I found this to be a defence frequently used across institutes when a trainer was challenged or a student failed to toe the line.

Staff conflict frequently appeared to be managed by the course director using the trainer's psychopathology to shame and control. Several trainers interviewed had been in therapy with the person who now "signed" their paycheque. Pathologising and scapegoating the other was an issue that arose time and time again, leading to the curious situation of psychotherapists whose skills lie in therapeutic relating and open communication, using their knowledge of the other's or their own history in order to close down communication. One trainer told me of his fear that a secret known only to the course director who used to be his therapist would be exposed if he challenged her openly in the team.

Observing trainers *in situ* I saw for myself the pressure on staff to toe the party line. I felt very much the outsider. I was struck by how frequently "coded" communication was present. This was used to communicate to each other concerns that could not be expressed to me. Frequently trainers in staff meetings seemed to be guarded and defensive, giving outwardly confident but woolly responses. The meetings seemed full of secrets and sidebars, often justified by the need to keep confidentiality. When something *was* identified as a problem, pathology was used to make meaning of it. This was usually directed at the students who were blamed for disharmony. Training groups were described as "difficult", "from hell", "my penance". I heard students referred to as "narcissistic", "borderline", and even pathologised for being "foreign" or "gay".

I found that the conflict between course directors and trainers centred around quality vs. quantity. As the choice about where to train as any particular kind of counsellor or psychotherapist increases institutes are having more difficulty in filling up their courses. In every institute I visited marketing policies and acceptance procedures were challenged (in private) by trainers who were put in the position of training students they thought were unsuitable. Trainers subsequently felt their hands were tied when it came to holding students back or failing them altogether. Students were only allowed to be deferred and deferred. No one was to fail. One trainer told me of a student who had just been "deferred" for the fourth time!

An alarming number of trainers told stories of students who had been reported to the course director for plagiarising and other forms of cheating on their final papers or exam tapes who went on to pass the next year. In more than one institute that has their courses validated by a universitiy trainers who were brave enough to bring these and other concerns to the university were sacked for various reasons that appeared to be "for their own good" and their concerns were never addressed.

The way forward

From these three interconnected areas of concern: management, culture and communication, I have drawn three shadow themes which run through each and I believe represent the basic instability in our places of learning:

- The shadow of power.
- The shadow of care.
- The shadow of emotional literacy.

These I believe are the unconscious dynamics within our institutional systems that create the muddles in the middle (see Chapter Seven) that need to be complained about, whilst at the same time creating the impossibility of this happening.

Power

The shadow of power is its misuse. This can happen when individuals are uninformed and overwhelmed. Passion, dedication and hard work are not enough to drown out the intoxicating effects of positive transference and idealisation. Leaders who can openly acknowledge and discuss their own their potential to abuse power are more likely to use their power creatively. I believe the key to a successful system and fulfilled staff is knowing when and how to withdraw so that others can be empowered and show their creativity. Management training and/or input from the corporate world could support the people at the top and relieve some of the pressures. This would help to develop more understanding of the need for the system to be held by both "male" and "female" strengths and would support clearer definition of roles, management of boundaries and open recruitment of both staff and students based on merit and experience. I believe that leaders in our organisations would also benefit from regular "mentoring" from another who has been in a position of power but with whom the leader is not in unspoken competition.

Care

Whether it sits comfortably with us or not, institutions seem to hold the relational construct of parent/child which becomes the basis of internalised interactions for trainer/trainee and trainee/client relationships. Institutes are not consciously aiming at infantilising the student but are attempting to create a healthy environment where adults meet together for the purposes of exchanging the experience of becoming or being a therapist. However, unconsciously, any learning group will mirror the family, and love and care as well as the potential for misuse and abuse are all powerful dynamics. The students will look to their trainers for care and attention. The shadow of care is neglect, abandonment, envy and greed. When our systems under stress we seem to abandon and/or neglect our standards in fighting for survival. Unequal rewards can invite envy and greed. We need systems in place to manage this such as good managerial support, monitoring of tutors' workloads, a culture of mutual respect, and the availability of leader and staff to hear and respond appropriately to students' anxieties and grievances.

Emotional literacy

Communication between everyone is vital and holds the system together as well as having the potential to fragment it. Our theoretical understanding and use of this in relationship connects us and divides us. Conflict, whether transparent or hidden, is inevitable. When under threat we defend ourselves in the best way we know how. The shadow side of emotional literacy is corrupt communication. In management I suggest we keep theory out of the room when business is done and keep the task of running the system as focal. I suggest that as tutors we reflect on the way we use our theoretical understanding in relationship with students and that we do not abuse this if we feel personally attacked.

Meetings seem most useful if frequent and there is time set aside for open dialogue. In my own institution I have introduced bi-monthly Sangha groups for the management team. These groups alternate with management meetings. Sangha is Buddhist terminology for a spiritual community group. These are not intended for Buddhist only followers but there is a mutual interest in the Buddhist concept of "mindfulness" as a vehicle for us to work transparently and productively together, minimising our group shadow.

Our Sangha groups are conducted in the Buddhist spirit of mindfulness (Nhat Hahn, 1987). Mindfulness is simply the energy that reminds us what is in front of us, and allows us, through its practice, to remain present with what *is*, exactly as it is, without trying to change it. This group space enables us to see each other as we are, to build trust and tolerance for our differences, and have more transparency in our interactions. If we have the permission to show our "madness" or "badness" my experience is that it becomes less toxic. My experience as a trainer and researcher is that what we say we do is not necessarily the reality of what we *are* doing. Mindfulness practice allows us, in a boundaried space, to challenge that and be still in a frantic world of busy-ness. Having a Sangha group is just one way. Our history as a group has been one where we have had to work together to make this happen effectively. Some members found the process threatening at first but struggled to stay with it. We have learnt that it works better when everyone is committed to the spirit of mindfulness and willing to share openly in the knowledge that this can take time, courage and patience.

Complaints procedures

For a profession whose lifeblood is healing in relationship, it seems surprising how little support there is for everyone when a complaint *is* made against a trainer, course director or examiner. Interestingly, although there is a systemic pull to pathologise trainees who speak out within the training group or who complain informally to the course director, trainers who *have* had complaints made against them report having felt frightened and marginalized. Several trainers reported that their trainees' formal complaints about their behaviour were treated as irritating by the course director in the staff group but were taken very seriously by that same course director when talking to the student involved, leaving the trainer feeling unsupported. Trainers who were later to see copies of correspondence to trainees who complained reported that the party line was, "Thank you for bringing this to our attention. We will certainly take it up with the trainer involved". This approach may be designed to by-pass a formal complaints procedure but it hardly makes trainers feel safe.

How we attend to everyone when they are dissatisfied or disillusioned matters. Investigating and managing complaints needs to be a collaborative process and speed is vital in order that people feel heard when it matters most to them and so that the original complaint does not escalate into something bigger than was originally intended.

I suggest that we need to develop a humanistic framework that embraces the principles of dialogue and restorative justice (Johnstone, 2003). The three principles behind restorative justice are: "Concern for the victim", "accountability and repair", and "engagement and participation", held within an over-arching attitude of respect.

There are different methods of using the principles of restorative justice. In my own organisation I have tried to implement this in relation to how we manage complaints and grievances. The Sangha groups provide the ground where the staff team can give time to the shadow in an atmosphere of mindfulness and acceptance of difference. For the management this creates an environment where support and challenge can happen in a different way, in the spirit of "witnessing" rather than issues escalating within and between people. I believe that what happens at the top will trickle down and influence the whole.

If a grievance *does* arise in the system staff and students are aware that a key person is available that day to listen and provide support. As "head" of the institute students know that I aim to be as available as possible and that I will return a phone call or email within twenty-four hours. This availability has not been misused by anyone during the period I have been in position. Two other senior tutors and a student mentor, who is one of our graduates, are also available and students may prefer to speak to one of them. Where a grievance or complaint is made the issue is discussed openly in the staff team in the spirit of "what happened" and "how, as a team can we understand this and improve our practice". Our aim is to maintain transparency, and fully attend with an over-arching attitude of concern and repair.

Whether the complainant is a student or a trainer, he is supported in speaking out and naming his concerns. I have found that most grievances are resolved at this point. Accountability and the psychological contract, or the unspoken expectations and assumptions that we all carry, are explored. The complainant and the person complained against are listened to and given support. After an initial meeting with a key person a further three-way meeting—if required—is set up as soon as it can be arranged. A way forward is then negotiated, dependent on the needs of the hurt party. To negotiate what needs to happen in the way of repair is in itself reparative. Everyone involved in the complaint is likely to feel under stress and possibly victimised. As trainers we would hope not to be defensive and to reflect in the staff team on the nature of the complaint and what it might teach us about improving our practice. Our experience in the Sangha group has helped us let go of the need to "be right". We aim to repair and work through rather than sideline, shame, blame or punish. This, in my opinion, is practising and modelling what we preach.

Conclusion

I have attempted here to show you some of my doctoral work towards uncovering shadow issues within our places of professional learning, and I have described my own attempts to address these in the organisation I run. I believe there is a need to have a conceptual framework for institutional complaints procedures that embraces both light and shadow, not just a list of rules and sanctions.

When I began my research into the culture of psychotherapy organisations Christmas was on the horizon and the Charles Dickens story of "A Christmas Carol" was on the television. In the story Scrooge appears to represent all that is shadow in his business. He is feared by all, and silences those beneath him. The story progresses with the ghost of Jacob Marley, Scrooge's previous business partner, paying Scrooge a visit. Marley tells him how he is doomed if the business continues as it is, and dares to awaken Scrooge to reality. Scrooge has lost sight of relationships and Marley invites him to reflect on his narcissistic ways. In a sense he holds up a mirror. Three ghosts of Past, Present and Future enable Scrooge to see firstly himself, and in doing that he is helped to see others. Finally he is connected, though those links, to humanity and humility. Gradually we see that Scrooge is not an evil man, just a man who has suffered himself and lost his way. We are shown that shadow and light are closely linked and how people can be damaged when denial of shadow is the culture. We are shown fear, suspicion, paranoia and shame.

The story is about losing sight of self, of relationship, the misuse of power and the complexities of the psyche. It is about a fixed, abusive culture that needs shaking up and awakening. Jacob Marley shows how he, previously as corrupt as Scrooge, gains insight. It is about transformation through the illumination of the shadow.

Scrooge was not a bad man but his mind was busy with other things, such as running a business, managing staff and counting the money. He forgot about his relationships with those he was responsible for. The parallel with psychotherapy institutes is clearly visible. As trainers, managers and psychotherapists perhaps we too have been too busy to look beneath the surface.

CHAPTER NINE

Intimacy, risk, and reciprocity in psychotherapy: intricate ethical challenges[1]

Tim Bond

This chapter is the outcome of a public dialogue at the 2005 World Transactional Analysis Conference in Edinburgh, between Bill Cornell and myself. Our conversation was facilitated by Sue Eusden, chairperson of the ethics committee of the Institute of Transactional Analysis (ITA) in the United Kingdom (UK) and Carol Shadbolt, a UK psychotherapist, with contributions from a distinguished audience. Writing this has provided me with the opportunity to digest the contributions of the participants and to integrate them within a longer-term project started five years ago in search of an ethic that will enrich and support our ethical mindfulness as we grapple with the intricate ethical challenges of routine psychotherapeutic practice.

One of the distinctive challenges for all approaches to psychotherapy is the psychologically intimate nature of the work. Our professional ethics to date have been primarily concerned with protecting the boundaries of the relationship so as to create a therapeutic space that is safe from unwelcome intrusion and strong enough to contain the interpersonal dynamics of the therapeutic process as well as to prevent the exploitation of clients in moments of vulnerability.

McGrath (1994) has demonstrated the application of ethical principles to determining appropriate boundaries concerning dual relationships, a perennial ethical challenge for all therapists. However, as someone who has been thinking about the ethics of our profession and other caring professions for 20 years, I have become increasingly interested in what our ethics do not address. For all sorts of laudable reasons, our collective professional ethics have been driven by a concern to set minimum standards for the safety of clients. Internationally, there are variations in the details of these standards in order to account for cultural context and differences between national legal requirements, but the concern over client safety appears to be a primary professional obligation that is universally recognized. This concern has been used to set the baseline for acceptable professional conduct and to provide the basis for investigating and disciplining professional behaviour that falls below that standard.

However, most therapy is delivered at levels above this minimum safety standard by therapists who are ethically conscientious and reasonably competent. If professional ethics become too exclusively preoccupied with the boundaries between good and bad practice, there is a risk that they become irrelevant once a therapist is securely above that line. I have always felt uneasy about this possibility as I see ethics as intrinsic and pervasive throughout therapy. All traditions of therapy are founded on and motivated by moral values and visions of the good life or, perhaps more accurately, a better life based on improved insight and healing. In addition to this therapeutic moral purpose, the client and therapist bring personal value positions with them into their relationship, and moral issues frequently arise during the course of therapy. Ethics thus extend far beyond concerns about client safety, important as this issue is.

I have been asking myself whether existing approaches to therapeutic ethics are an adequate basis for routine therapeutic work by ethically conscientious and reasonably competent therapists. What is missing? What remains problematic? To determine what is missing requires some attempt to say what an optimum professional ethic ought to provide. I think it is realistic to expect ethics that are primarily designed to inform and support practice to have the following characteristics:

1. Sufficiently encompassing of the variety and complexity of situations that arise in practice to be a useful source of support for the practitioner.

2. Simple enough to be both readily recalled by busy practitioners during the course of their work and readily communicable to others, including clients.

3. Provide a moral lens that brings critical issues into sharper focus.

4. Offer a moral compass to assist therapists to navigate the moral terrain of their work by providing reference points from which to consider ethical challenges and dilemmas.

When viewed against these criteria, many approaches to professional ethics are deficient in four closely related aspects that are particularly relevant to the relational tradition in therapy.

First, they do not address the ongoing tension between attending to client safety and the risk taking by both clients and therapists that is required for therapy to be effective. At its simplest, how should a therapist offer a risky intervention for therapeutic purposes? In varying degrees, this is a recurrent challenge in every therapeutic relationship. To be totally risk avoidant is to be ineffective and to collude with existing patterns that have become problematic.

A closely related challenge is the unavoidable uncertainty when working within a dynamic process in which both client and therapist are reflexively repositioning themselves in response to the other's contribution. The therapeutic process unfolds successively rather than being predictable from the outset. Following Sullivan, Stern (1998) observed, "Tolerance of uncertainty and ambiguity are built into the clinical practice of detailed inquiry" (pp. 602–603). Risk and uncertainty are inescapable existential challenges that face all therapists and their clients, and since they are often only partially and inadequately addressed in existing approaches to ethics, they merit further consideration.

Two other challenges that arise in all therapies may also be at their most evident in relational traditions. The first of these relational challenges concerns working across significant differences between people with sufficient understanding of the other person's experience and frames of reference. The second is how to take into account the inequality of power and influence within the therapeutic relationship. The psychologically intimate nature of therapy makes it particularly sensitive to issues of difference and inequality in ways in which the client is obviously vulnerable, but, perhaps less obviously, the therapist may also become vulnerable in the reciprocal manoeuvring of the ongoing relationship. The maxim that "there is no intimacy without reciprocity" (Oakley, 2005, p. 226) has been influential in contemporary social sciences concerned with understanding people in qualitative depth and promoting human emancipation.

The corollary of the aforementioned maxim is that there is "no reciprocity without mutual vulnerability". The fact is that the therapist also risks being changed for better or worse by the encounter. This mutual vulnerability arises from the combination of the inescapable relational challenges of difference and inequality and the existential challenges of risk and uncertainty. Issues around client safety can probably only be adequately dealt with by reference to extrinsic points of reference—such as rationally and analytically justified principles—if they are to be publicly credible beyond the profession. In contrast, the mutual vulnerabilities of therapy are intrinsic to therapy and perhaps need a different register and tone so as to create ethical points of reference for working within the therapeutic relationship. For the last 5 years I have been considering different ways of constructing an intrinsic ethical framework that could be useful in developing and supporting the ethical commitment of well-intentioned and competent therapists throughout their work.

A missing ethic?

At first glance, the notion of a missing ethic may seem offensive to some, especially those who have invested considerable efforts in developing or learning existing ethics for psychotherapy. In addition, the implication that the psychotherapy profession is based on an incomplete ethic may seem profoundly troubling to others. I am, in many ways, a reluctant advocate of the possibility of a missing ethic because I also share these reservations. In fact, I have been actively involved in leading the development of the ethical infrastructure for the British Association for Counselling and Psychotherapy (BACP), a professional body with about 25,000 members. Along the way, I developed a systematic approach to an ethic of respect for individual autonomy (Bond, 1993), became progressively convinced of the wisdom of holding several ethical principles alongside each other (Bond, 2000), led the change from rule-based ethics to a principle-based system and promoting ethical mindfulness in professional practice (British Association for Counselling and Psychotherapy, 2002) and research (Bond, 2004), and have been active in researching contextually appropriate ethics both within the UK and internationally through the International Association for Counselling.

I might not have come to the conclusions that I am about to offer had I not also been actively involved in teaching the philosophical basis of qualitative research and research ethics in the highest achieving department of educational studies in Britain. The quest for researching and enriching qualitative data poses many philosophical and technical difficulties that have parallels to the challenges faced by psychotherapists in responding to psychological intimacy and reciprocity. Most importantly for this article, these experiences in educational studies provided me with another point of reference that freed me from the constraints of a single professional discourse. The renaissance of interest in relational approaches evident at the 2005 World Transactional Analysis Conference is taking place in other therapeutic traditions as well as more widely in the social sciences and associated professions.

The tipping point that led me to commit to examining the possibility of a re-conceptualised ethic of trust occurred in Auckland, New Zealand, in 2002. I had arrived tired and barely recovered from jet lag to begin a lecture tour and to facilitate workshops, some of which were co-facilitated with a distinguished Maori elder. A Maori greeting could not be more different from the English reserve that I had regressed to under the pressure of travel. The traditional Maori way of greeting strangers is to offer a fierce challenge as a way of provoking visitors to present themselves and declare what they are about. I was thus greeted by an elderly lady with an air of authority based on generations of traditional wisdom outside my cultural experience. As she leaned on an impressive and perhaps slightly threatening wooden stick, she opened our first conversation with, "So, you are big in ethics. Tell me! What is the one most important thing in ethics?" My usual answer to ethical questions is to seek further information about the motivation and circumstances behind the question. But this seemed too limp a response to such an unexpected challenge. I had travelled for almost 2 days preoccupied with the question that had now been posed so forcefully. What had eluded my conscious ruminations emerged unexpectedly from my subconscious and I heard myself responding, "Trust".

Later, when I reflected on my answer, I realized that unlike the principle of autonomy, which probably is only meaningful to about a third of the world's population—those with individualized notions of self, particularly in North America, Western Europe, and the English-speaking countries in the southern hemisphere—trust is a more universal point of ethical reference. Issues of trust apply just as well to people whose primary unit of ethical concern is an extended family or tribe. The ubiquity of "trust" as a human concern makes it more portable across cultural differences but perhaps also more problematic, because trust and being trustworthy take many different forms according to the macrocultural context and the microdynamics of a specific relationship at a specific place and time.

Etymologically, the word "trust" was probably introduced into the English language from the Old Norse "traust" (Trumble & Stevenson, 2002) during the diaspora of the Vikings, a time that led to their occupation of most of the northern and western lands in the British Isles during the ninth century A.D. Trust was a virtue that was named and valued in the heroic social ethos of a warrior culture represented in the Sagas and the didactic poetic wisdom of the Hávamál. As such, it may seem the unlikely source of an ethic for psychotherapy, that is, until one perceives the work as resolving current psychological and interpersonal conflict or the consequences of past conflicts. Trust and mistrust, risk and safety are just as present as issues in psychotherapy today as they were in a more self-consciously warrior culture.

The potential of an ethic of trust

The primary meaning of trust as a noun is "faith or confidence in the loyalty, strength, veracity etc., of a person or thing" (Trumble & Stevenson, 2002). For therapy to work, both therapist and client require a degree of reciprocal trust in each other that is sufficient to enable the work to proceed. The level of trust may vary depending on the degree of intimacy and difficulty encountered in the work, but it needs to be sufficient. Too little trust and the work stalls, becomes stuck, or fails completely. Working directly with the relationship as it forms between therapist and client is perhaps one of the most personally exposing and psychologically intimate ways of working for both individuals involved. Working within the relational tradition both requires and promotes a correspondingly high level of trust within a context that also evokes anxiety and mistrust.

However, the ethic of trust has a long history in professional ethics, one that has sometimes been quite problematic in both meaning and application. When I started training as a mental welfare officer and social worker in the 1970s, it was commonplace to hear doctors say to an anxious or querulous patient, "Trust me. I am a doctor". There are many potential interpretations of this phrase, but at the time, I think that patients heard it, according to the doctor's tone of voice, as either well-intended reassurance if they were anxious so they would not ask further fearful questions (based on the idea that what is not said can be repressed or better contained) or as a rebuff to silence them if they were complaining. The statement "Trust me. I am a doctor" places both patient and doctor within an ethic of paternalistic beneficence that retains professional autonomy for the doctor and, at its most extreme, demands the silent compliance of the patient. This contamination of trust with compliance ultimately discredited trust as a credible professional ethic. It had instead become a unilateral ethic vulnerable to abuse by the power holder. In fact, the 1960s and 1970s saw a succession of exposés of questionable medical practice. In the United Kingdom, several hundred unethical medical experiments were reported under the title "Human Guinea Pigs" (Pappworth, 1967), and shortly afterward, in the United States the Tuskegee syphilis experiment, which had been running since the 1930s, was finally exposed in the New York Times in 1972 and closed down (Jonsen, 1999). These and many other examples of questionable ethical practice in the most respected of professions created a justifiable cynicism concerning professional ethics founded on trust.

A political and ethical discourse on rights was emerging at about the same time. This became the basis of another form of unilateral ethics based on patient autonomy and a steadily increasing emphasis on informed consent. Giving the patient the ultimate right to consent to or veto a treatment remains an essential safeguard against the worst excesses of exploitation, although this has proved ethically insufficient in a number of significant ways. First, no amount of elaboration in the requirements to ensure that the recipient of services is adequately informed and that consent is freely given can wholly redress the imbalance of power derived from professional influence and expertise or alleviate the pressures on someone in need of help to accept what is on offer as better than nothing. Second, the strategy deployed to protect service users' rights can equally be used to disempower them, particularly if something goes wrong. "The risks were explained to you and you consented to them in order to receive that treatment" is a fairly typical response if the client later protests some aspect of treatment. Consent is thus a two-edged sword that can cut both ways: at the professional prospectively and at the service user retrospectively. Third, a hypothetical risk that might occur in the future weighs much more lightly than an immediate need. It is difficult to anticipate how one might feel in the future about events that have not yet happened in comparison to the urgency and power of immediate experience.

Onora O'Neill, a prominent British bio-ethicist, is a forceful critic of the over-reliance on consent as an ethical panacea and has argued for revival of trust as an essential ethic. She suggests that over-formalizing procedures designed to promote trust creates a regression to mistrust. The very steps that are designed to make trust less necessary have the effect of making trust less achievable, so the anxieties persist (O'Neill, 2002, p. 131). At the risk of oversimplifying her argument, it is not possible to resolve a relational problem by instrumental solutions such as the technology of consent or a generalized ethic of individual autonomy. The solution to mistrust is relational and local. I understand O'Neill to be advocating trust as a bilateral ethic requiring the commitment of both parties. However, as a political philosopher, she is more interested in the implications of these ideas for public life and service infrastructure than in defining how trust might operate in psychologically intimate relationships like psychotherapy or how trust might operate as a local and relational ethic.

A revived ethic of trust for the talking therapies

In my own work as a therapist and supervisor, I have watched myself and other therapists adopt an ethic of respect for client autonomy as an improvement on an ethic of paternalistic fidelity. In the close-up work of psychotherapy and counselling, an ethic of autonomy remains a useful point of external reference for analysing the rights and responsibilities of the parties to the therapeutic relationship in a detached and rational way. It is an ethic that is particularly meaningful to clients whose culture incorporates a Westernised ethic of self-government, the literal meaning of autonomy. However, its strength is also its weakness. The discourse of rights and responsibilities associated with an ethic of autonomy underestimates the significance of relationship both in general and more specifically. In general, it underestimates that both the therapist's and client's well-being depend on a network of relationships outside the room. Specifically, it underestimates the significance of the quality of the relationship between the therapist and the client rather than focusing on them as two separate and bounded people. The robustness of an extrinsic ethic of autonomy directs attention to the lack of an equivalent ethic that is intrinsic to the work with a specific client, an ethic that is relational, local, and capable of fostering ethically mindful practice, especially for therapies that are psychologically intimate and require reciprocity between therapist and client.

All psychotherapies are psychologically intimate on the client's part and to varying degrees on the therapist's part. Building and sustaining a therapeutic relationship, even for the most behavioural or cognitive therapist, involves some degree of relational reciprocity. The active use of congruence in person-centred approaches or relational dynamics in a variety of therapies, such as object relations, gestalt, or transactional analysis, require high levels of reciprocity on the part of the therapist as well as the client.

As I have reflected on what might constitute an intrinsic ethic, I have been influenced by ideas about the way different human interests require different rationalities (Habermas, 1986), the relational mysticism of Buber (1957/1970), the philosophy of Levinas (Peperzak, Critchley, Bernasconi, 1996), and post-modern ethics (Bauman, 1993, 1994). The challenge has been how to move beyond the more abstract, often inspirational, and certainly thought-provoking writing of philosophers to a way of representing a revived ethic of trust that meets the four criteria described in the opening section of this article. After a process of trial and error, public discussions on three continents, and professional reflection, I have approached trust as a reciprocal relationship that by implication requires the ethical commitment and mindfulness of all parties to that relationship. This relationship exists in counterpoise to the challenges that are found in many types of helping relationships but especially the psychological intimacy and vulnerability of psychotherapy. It is dynamic and embodied rather than rational and abstract. The quality and strength of the relationship is determined experientially rather than analytically and is evaluated in dialogue between those directly involved (typically therapists and clients), but it may also be supported by others from their respective communities.

An ethic of trust is defined as one that supports the development of reciprocal relationships of sufficient strength to withstand the relational challenges of difference and inequality and the existential challenges of risk and uncertainty. Each of these ethical challenges occurs in different ways in psychotherapy.

Difference

Difference between people poses significant challenges in human relationships in general. Belonging and shared identity as a social unit is strongly associated with sameness. Difference sets people apart from the group, especially in times of collective stress, unless the group has the wisdom to recognize the ways in which differences can enrich and strengthen its resourcefulness. Difference may elicit forceful, even bullying responses to enforce conformity, including prejudice and unfair treatment, rejection, exclusion, and abandonment. Difference is so often a cause of hurt that clients are justifiably fearful of revealing differences that deviate from the perceived social norm or the norms communicated by the therapist. The psychological intimacy of the encounter increases the potential vulnerability of the client to a negative reaction by the therapist. The therapist also faces distinctive challenges to listening beyond his or her own life experience. These challenges are substantial when the listening is across major obvious differences in experience, such as life stages, gender, ethnicity, culture, or religion. This tests the therapist's knowledge, capacity for eliciting relationship-forming information and/or therapeutic curiosity, and empathic imagination in order to form the basis of a therapeutic relationship in which the client feels sufficiently understood to want to undertake the challenges of change. Difference is thus a source of vulnerability for both client and therapist, an obvious potential source of misunderstanding and alienation in the sense of both "making a stranger" and provoking "emotional distancing".

Inequality

Within the therapeutic relationship there are intrinsic and extrinsic sources of inequality. The extrinsic ones are unlikely to be resolved by therapy, certainly in the short term or by therapy alone, but they will be present as an influence on the dynamics of the relationship. These are inequalities arising from the social structure of society and the unequal distribution of power and status as well as from personal achievement. Class, wealth, education, occupation, and other social factors are part of the daily realities of both the therapist and client outside the therapy room, but they are also likely to be present within it as part of the background against which the therapeutic relationship is formed.

Intrinsic to the therapeutic relationship are the inherent differences in status and power between the person seeking help and the person offering help. Typically, the therapist is credited with greater knowledge, expertise, and psychological health by the client, who is disadvantaged by the vulnerability for which help is being sought. From a position of vulnerability, the client may have a vested interest, at least initially, in amplifying and idealizing the therapist's characteristics by imbuing the therapist with an exaggerated power to heal. Therapists work with these idealizations in many different ways. The metaphor of the "wounded healer" may be partially inspired by some therapists' egalitarian instincts to redress the power imbalance by reducing the power differentials based on fantasies of what it means to be healthy. Some clients are severely disadvantaged in terms of power and influence within the therapeutic relationship because of their difficulty in escaping the limitations of their psychological/interpersonal problems.

One aspect of the therapeutic relationship that may lead to potential inequalities is the power of experience. With all the other power vectors tending to favour the therapist, a therapist's experience may tend to predominate and become the point of reference, however it is translated and subtly communicated within the therapeutic model.

When experiential power flows from the therapist to the client, it carries the potential for healing and new learning. But the flow is not just one way. The quality of the attention given to the client's experience in psychotherapy also leaves the therapist highly exposed to being influenced by those experiences. This is especially true if the content is overtly disturbing or traumatizing or is communicated more covertly through the dynamics of the relationship. It may, in fact, only be available in transferences and countertransferences or other dynamics played out through the therapeutic relationship. When approached with humility, the therapist may be the beneficiary of new learning and even healing as a result of his or her exposure to the client's experiences. Occasionally, the therapist will be sufficiently discomforted to suffer varying degrees of experiential reflux; this can lead to self-doubt as a healthy response, deskilling as a more profound response, or secondary traumatisation as a potentially more disturbing and disabling response. The underlying question with experiential power is whose experience will colonize the other's by becoming the predominant point of reference? The therapist's task is to strive for a positive outcome, but both individuals will be changed by the encounter. Experiential power, once engaged, is always reciprocal.

Risk

Professional ethics struggle with risk. Risk involves being exposed to danger and/or the possibility of loss, injury, or some other adverse event (Trumble & Stevenson, 2002). With regard to psychotherapy, the reassuring version is that risks are controlled and/or eliminated from therapy. This position fits a risk-avoidant culture and may be suggested as a humane response by those who seek to reassure already vulnerable people who may be potential clients. The difficulty with this approach is that it is fundamentally dishonest and existentially infantilising. Professionally, it may lead to dysfunctionally defensive practice that prioritises the therapist's self-protection over being therapeutically effective. Risk is unavoidable in therapy just as it is in much of life. The challenge is how to represent the level of risk in a reasonably honest way. The obvious risks to the client involve time, economic resources, emotional investment, and the potential for harm. These have corresponding risks for the therapist. These risks for both client and therapist are, to a considerable extent, adequately addressed in the ethical discourse about the principles and practices around contracting. However, the relational representation of risk requires a more dialectical approach. One task is to construct a positive relationship in which the client feels understood, but if this is all that is achieved in therapy, the outcome may be to collude with what is troubling or dysfunctional for that person. The other task is to use the relationship as the basis for taking risks in order to achieve therapeutic changes (Cornell & Bonds-White, 2001/2005). This represents the dialectic that psychotherapists need to maintain a stance that incorporates two different modes of intention toward the client: one being to facilitate a deepening elaboration of the client's subjective experience and the other being to disturb and deconstruct it.

Heroic cultures, such as the Viking culture from which the word "trust" originated, glorified risk taking as a way of testing and proving oneself. Professional ethics for the talking therapies need to find some support from this positive attitude to risk taking in order to celebrate and validate the courage involved in seeking to heal one's wounds and to overcome the sense of vulnerability in the psychologically intimate process of therapy. The metaphor of the "wounded healer" that finds such resonance in therapy is, in part, a message of hope: that the discomfort and risk taking in therapy brings healing and that the therapist has travelled this journey ahead of the client and is therefore sufficiently knowledgeable to act as a reliable guide.

The challenge in professional ethics is to present risk taking in a way that is proportionate to the potential benefits and dangers. There is something between risk aversion and risk amplification that is an existentially more accurate representation of both how therapy works and what is relationally and psychologically healthy. Therapy models the interplay between trust and risk in the reciprocal dance between therapist and client as the therapeutic process unfolds. Risk taking is as unavoidable in therapy as it is in life.

Uncertainty

Therapy is full of uncertainty, and living with it at different levels is one of the existential challenges of the therapeutic process faced by therapist and client alike. One function of therapeutic models may be to act as a security blanket to mask some of the uncertainties while bringing a sense of direction and purpose to the therapeutic encounter.

One of the ways people seek to overcome uncertainty is by creating knowledge that provides understanding and control. Valued knowledge within a modern society is typically scientific, which is often presented as certainty even though it is always provisional because a new observation may disprove what was previously believed to be true (Popper, 1959). Therapeutic knowledge is similarly provisional both at the macro level of theoretical generalization and at the micro level of finding knowledge that is both true and useful within a specific therapeutic relationship. One of the tasks of being therapeutically trustworthy is neither to overstate certainty nor to descend into a state of nihilism by exaggerating uncertainty; the goal, instead, is to actively engage with producing local knowledge that is functional within the therapeutic relationship.

Coping with uncertainty is part of the therapeutic trajectory to recovery. Some of the most psychologically damaged people become so frightened of change that they prefer to stay in a familiar world of pain and turmoil. They are sufficiently comforted by the familiar and terrified of the unfamiliar that they are unable or unwilling to make the imaginative leap to what might be better. It was in an early transactional analysis training that I was first introduced to the concept of "payoffs", which reinforce staying stuck in familiar patterns (Berne, 1972). Perhaps because it kick-started my own therapy, this concept has continued to inform my own practice by directing attention to the relational valences at work inside and outside therapy. I have also found that it requires therapeutic judgment to use it effectively and in a trustworthy manner. Used without sound judgment and skill, it can reinforce self-blame and shame and add to the incapacitating forces on the client and possibly the therapist. From personal experience, I can testify that the ideas associated with payoffs can be extremely beneficial. However, there must always be a degree of uncertainty about the interplay between the therapeutic relationship that has been constructed and the intervention. The intrinsic uncertainty of the work requires the therapist to be watchful and vigilant with regard to unanticipated or unintended effects. It also "requires a certain type of humility in the therapist that she be prepared to learn from her client, allowing herself to be affected by the impact upon her and accepting that she may not necessarily know or understand immediately what is going on" (Cornell & Hargaden, 2005, p. 10).

Perhaps the most obvious source of uncertainty in any process of change is the difficulty of anticipating how one will feel when change is attained. The client is most vulnerable in this, but there is reciprocal uncertainty for the therapist as well. For example, a client's sense of emerging resilience and strength may lead to more challenging and discomforting exchanges within the therapy. One way the therapist demonstrates that he or she is trustworthy is to have the reciprocal resilience and strength to withstand the attack and to engage with it without subverting its therapeutic potential. Both therapist and client are engaged in a reciprocal process that cannot be wholly controlled by either the therapist or the client, and, as a consequence, both will encounter moments of uncertainty with varying degrees of profundity as the process unfolds.

To illustrate the application of an ethic of trust in therapy, I offer here some examples given by contributors to the public discussion at the 2005 World Transactional Analysis Conference.

Example 1: psychotherapy with gay men and lesbians

Sexuality, and sexual orientation in particular, are contentious issues within most societies, and not surprisingly, views on them differ within the therapeutic community. Intolerance of differences in sexual orientation is still frequently the norm in most parts of the world, and engagement with difference even in more liberal societies is often fairly superficial. The protection of individual rights from oppression by the majority is probably most effectively defended on the basis of robust universal human and civil rights. An intrinsic ethic of trust addresses different issues. It challenges both therapists and clients to reflect on their own similarities and divergences in values and life experience and how this impacts on such a psychologically intimate way of working as therapy. How is the quality of the relationship influenced by the life experience and values of those involved? What inequalities and differences do those individuals bring to the relationship? What are the risks of therapy between people with different values or life experiences or arising from differences in experiential power between the people involved? With regard to such potentially sensitive issues, uncertainty may not be a negative factor. In fact, dogmatic certainty may foreclose dialogue, whereas uncertainty may offer the space for meaningful interaction. Nevertheless, the question remains significant: what is the impact of uncertainty on the relationship? The ethic of trust directs attention to the relational implications of each of these questions for the people most directly affected rather than to a quest for a definitive view of who is right or what the authoritative position is on such intimate and potentially contentious topics.

Shadbolt's (2004) recent article on "Homophobia and Gay Affirmative Transactional Analysis" challenges all therapists to reflect on the relational dimension of the work in much greater depth than is typical. It raises two issues that are particularly relevant to an ethic of trust. The first concerns the impact of received cultural values on therapy; the second highlights the relational implications of the therapeutic model being used.

The influence of culture is pervasive throughout our lives in ways that are difficult to see from within, ways that frequently only become apparent when standing at a distance and viewing the familiar from a different cultural position. In her article, Shadbolt assumes that the therapist is willing to be supportive of gay and lesbian people, but she challenges the depth of that commitment and invites readers to question their assumptions about their adequacy to provide therapy. The intended reader is not someone who is antagonistic to homosexual identity and behaviour but a person with the kind of a liberal disposition that is increasingly typical of the therapeutic community in Westernised English-speaking societies. The article challenges superficial tolerance by illustrating the depth of the bias in favour of heterosexuality that is built into social structures and culture. Even the therapist's well-intentioned comments and/or actions may inadvertently add authority to such prejudices in the sense that certain matters are already judged and decided before the dialogue takes place. For example, Shadbolt invites us to imagine questioning a friend's heterosexual sexual orientation in the way that homosexuals are frequently questioned:

• When did you discover that you were heterosexual?
• Do you remember the first time you came out as heterosexual?

- Have you told your parents that you are heterosexual? How did they react?
- Do you ever feel like attempting suicide because you are hetero-sexual?

The preposterous nature of these questions demonstrates how cer-tain assumptions prevail and are reinforced within the cultural dis-courses of the dominant position; they also reveal the discomfort of standing outside those culturally supported positions. Thus, the depth of the relational challenge posed by difference and cultural inequality is exposed. Therapists cannot be neutral with regard to sexuality, but they can be self-aware. In transactional analysis this might involve examining the influence of the Cultural Parent (Drego, 1983) or the internalised "right way to be" within subsets of the Child ego state (Hargaden & Sills, 2002). But is self-awareness sufficient?

Later in her article, Shadbolt asks whether a therapist needs to share the same sexual orientation as the client in order to meet that person's needs. This is particularly relevant to an ethic of trust. It raises the question of what the impact of life experience and experi-ential power is on the relationship. A corollary of this question is whether good intentions alone are sufficient to meet an individual's therapeutic needs concerning sexual identity. I have tended toward a positive answer to this question provided the therapist has the appropriate humility to realize what he or she does not know and to approach the work in an open-minded way.

However, one strand of Shadbolt's argument caused me to reconsider my position. In discussing various views on the topic, she cites Lapworth (2003), who draws heavily on the work of Kohut to suggest that for therapy regarding sexual identity to be effective, the client and therapist need to have the same sexual orientation. This argument is based on Kohut's explanation of how therapy works, in particular, his three self-object transferences: mirroring, idealizing, and twinship (Kohut, 1984). Kohut suggested that a failure to meet any of these needs early in life has corresponding harmful effects later, although these may be redressed in therapy. Mirroring for young children involves communicating pleasure about their pres-ence and uniqueness; it is an uncontaminated reflection of the child back to himself or herself. The idealizing transference requires a powerful, calm, knowledgeable other to identify with in order to gradually internalise a self-soothing, self-containing, self-confident self. In the twinship transference, the client needs to have a sense of being like others, to share common ground; this validates a sense of belonging and connectedness.

For Lapworth, a therapist whose sexual orientation differs from that of the client would struggle to fulfil these tasks because of differences in identity. In his view, idealization requires "someone who can demonstrate the power, calm and experiential knowledge of being gay" because clients in the process of coming to terms with their sexuality need "to be inspired, mirrored and protected by another of the same sexuality who can be gradually internalised and developed into that part of the self which as Kohut saw it, has a fourfold purpose—as the repository of the ideals which guide our lives, the part of our self that controls our impulses, the part that can soothe ourselves in times of hurt or stress and lastly is the sense of humour, empathy, creativity and wisdom" (Lapworth, 2003).

The difficulties are even greater with regard to twinship transference. Such transference requires sufficient common ground to validate a sense of belonging and connectedness that enables the client "to experience and accept her true sexual self for herself and in relation to others" (Lapworth, 2003). Although this forms only a small part of a multifaceted article by Shadbolt (2004), I have selected this passage as one that raises significant questions for the therapist and that gains extra significance when viewed through the lens of an ethic of trust. According to Lapworth's analysis, difference in sexual orientation would be a barrier to acting as a good therapist. Shadbolt agrees that it is difficult to see how a heterosexual therapist, however empathic, can provide the affirmation and acceptance required by a gay or lesbian client given the lack of sameness in sexual orientation and identity. The level of risk for the client and secondarily for the therapist would be sufficient to frustrate the therapy or, at worst, harm a fragile and emergent identity.

After reading and discussing Shadbolt's ideas at the 2005 World Transactional Analysis Conference, I have found myself reengaging with the issue of what it means to be trustworthy as a therapist when working with issues of sexual orientation and identity. My own sexuality and identity are not easily polarized as either heterosexual or homosexual, so the dichotomous assumptions of the

extracts I have taken from what Shadbolt wrote do not exactly capture the dilemmas I personally face in working with clients.
However, they do challenge me to review at what point a client's
sexual orientation and identity are so different from my own that I
may not be able to help effectively. In my case, the wholly homosexual or wholly heterosexual client with a good deal invested in maintaining a singular orientation might be more problematic if the work
required us to undertake Kohut's therapeutic tasks. The intrinsic
trust required in therapy requires me to make this personal link
rather than to think in depersonalised and generalized terms.

This illustrates well the way in which trust and mistrust in therapy are relational and specific to the people involved. The intrinsic
ethic of trust challenges me to consider how I might incorporate new
insights about a familiar issue in my therapeutic work. I hope that I
can approach my next client to whom this applies with sufficient
humility to want to discuss some of these ideas at an appropriate
point in our work so as to engage him or her in a dialogue about what
he or she wants. An ethic of trust not only provides points of reference
that reinforce the reciprocal nature of the therapeutic relationship as it
unfolds, but it also emphasizes the value of dialogue as a way of
resolving equivocal therapeutic and ethical issues such as these.

Example 2: using a risky intervention

The issue of risk in therapy presents a perennial challenge for all
therapists. It is so commonplace that it probably occurs several times
in some sessions and many times a day for a busy therapist. In our
exchange of e-mails in preparation for the public dialogue about this
issue at the conference, Sue Eusden (personal communication, 2 July,
2005) wrote about her sense of the ethical implications of the "gap"
between herself and her client:

> "The gap is an intersubjective space. It is the space between my
> client and me. It is also the space between my intention in mak-
> ing an intervention and how the other receives it. It is in this gap
> that an intervention aimed to be transformative can be experi-
> enced as abusive or "unethical". Hence, as we mind the gap, we
> can only do so in a relational sense. If I believe that I can manage
> or mind the gap, then I am at risk of operating arelationally and
> losing contact with my client. I believe this is when I begin to

operate at the edge of ethical thinking as I assume a one-up position over my client. Minding the gap is, for me, about attending to my interventions and their impact as well as staying exquisitely curious about what emerges and available to explore the dynamic disturbance that may unfold. I believe mistakes are a potentially vital part of our work: vital in the sense of alive making. Such moments in therapy need to be deeply underpinned by ethical thinking and questioning on behalf of the therapist."

Drawing on her own experience as a therapist and her work on professional conduct for the ITA ethics committee, Eusden has found that what comes to be viewed as unethical is not necessarily undertaken out of ill intent toward the client or as an act of recklessness or negligence. Rather, it is evaluated as unethical because of a persistent neglect of the relational dimension and lack of attention to the intricacies to which an ethic of trust directs our attention:

"In my view, I may act unethically often in my practice, not through gross misconduct, but more through inattention, going for an easy option at times, or making poor interventions. Such moments may be experienced as ineffectual at best and abusive at worst. What brings such choices to the attention of an ethics committee is often the therapist's inattention to the gap followed by defensiveness around exploring ethical implications between himself or herself and the client in an exquisitely curious way that accounts for the vulnerability and intersubjectivity of both individuals. Instead, the therapist might move to a shame-based response to authority or accusation.

One frame of reference in transactional analysis suggests that a mistake made by the therapist represents his or her counter-transferential move in a game. This might be the therapist's con or gimmick. Some may see this as a co-created aspect of the relationship. Here trust involves an interesting tension. Do the two individuals have enough trust in each other and/or the process to continue exploring, or is the trust disrupted at this point?"
[S. Eusden, personal communication, 2 July, 2005]

Trust is thus not risk avoidance but a matter of:

- Awareness that a risk has been taken.
- Careful observation of the consequences, elegantly and evocatively described by the phrase "exquisite curiosity".

- Dialogue and evaluation with the client from a position of non-defensive security on the part of the therapist.
- Offering a relational remedy for any unwanted effects and substituting or reframing the intervention according to the therapeutic circumstances.
- Sustaining the therapeutic flow in dialogue with the client.
- Heightened ethical awareness and engagement throughout the therapeutic process.

Bill Cornell, (2003) provided the following example of how mistakes need not lead to unethical consequences and can become the source of positive therapeutic outcomes. The adverse reaction of the client required that the therapist exercise considerable insight and skill so as to remain therapeutic and to regain the client's trust.

> "Our work together almost collapsed when I double-booked her session after a vacation. Even though I owned the mistake as mine and the other client agreed to come back at another time, Suzanne felt that I had humiliated her and that this was clear evidence that I did not care and wanted to be rid of her. In Suzanne's mind it seemed perfectly obvious that she had somehow become a bore or a burden to me. It seemed better to leave than be angry with me.
>
> This mistake on my part and Suzanne's reaction to it became a pivotal moment in her therapy. It was clear to her that we were both extremely uncomfortable in the face of my error, but I did not get rid of her. She could see that I could tolerate my own discomfort and maintain an investment in her well-being. This provided her with an emotional space within which we could examine all of her various reactions. She was able to begin to see that the only way she could understand my mistake was as a desire to be rid of her, that this habitual explanation was an expression of her script that imposed a particular meaning on what had happened. If this meaning were accurate, it made sense that she (as usual) should prepare to leave yet another important place of hope in her life and yet again to go it alone". [p. 8]

The insight gained from this accidentally therapeutic moment enabled the therapy to proceed with both therapist and client discomforted but wiser. Perhaps most importantly, trust was actively maintained at a level that sustained the ongoing relationship in order to overcome the risk created by the client's initial sense of hurt. Thus, trust outweighed risk and the client's uncertainty about proceeding with the therapy.

Trust: a new ethic to eclipse the old?

This chapter offers an exploratory exposition of the potential of a re-conceptualised ethic of trust, one designed to take on the intricate challenges of intimacy and reciprocity in psychotherapy, especially psychotherapy informed by the relational tradition. There is no sug-gestion that the intrinsic ethic of trust should replace an extrinsic ethic of principles. Both are social constructs hewn with different cultural tools for different purposes in the sense of offering alterna-tive perspectives. Both become dysfunctional and would support unethical behaviour when misapplied, and both may strain to achieve their purpose even when appropriately applied to complex ethical issues. What I hope an ethic of trust might reasonably be expected to achieve—after further refinement through dialogue of the type that took place in the 2005 World Transactional Analysis Conference—is to:

- Reinvigorate engagement with the topic of ethics, especially for those practitioners who are competent and ethically minded, by providing a way of engaging with the intricate issues that per-vade therapy.

- Bring the discourses of therapy and ethics closer together in ways that enable them to be used in more sophisticated ways in the quest for the "good life" and as part of the therapeutic trajectory for moving from an impaired life toward an attainable version of the good-enough life.

- Direct attention to the relational virtue of trust as reciprocal between therapist and client and thus a shared ethic to which both contribute, even though the therapist will at times be responsible for facilitating and protecting the therapeutic space in which trust may flourish.

- Reinforce the value of dialogue within the therapeutic relation-ship and with the communities of support available to both therapist and client to resolve ethical issues and dilemmas.

A relational ethic of trust is not intended to eclipse the ethical principles set out by writers such as Thompson (1990), McGrath (1994), myself (BACP, 2002; Bond, 2000), and many others. The ethic of trust is supplementary to these and has yet to be put to the test to see if it can function as an operational professional ethic. I welcome feedback and copies of material that cite this approach to ethics.

NOTE

1. This article was originally published in the April 2006 issue of the *Transactional Analysis Journal*, Volume 36, Number 2, and it is republished with permission of the International Transactional Analysis Association and the author.

Initial therapy agreement

This agreement expresses the commitment each of us makes at the outset. Please read it through when you have time, as we will discuss things further next week. Once we have discussed and agreed the details, we will both sign and keep one copy to register our shared understanding.

1. We have agreed to meet at (time)__ each _(day)_. This is "your time" each week that I have set aside for you. Each session lasts one hour. It is important for effective therapy that we try to maintain a regular and continuous commitment. If a change of circumstance makes this difficult for you, we can discuss the possibility of a different date and time and I will do my best to rearrange things if I can.

2. The fee we have agreed is £__ per one hour session. Fees are due each session/on the last session of each month. (or other arrangements by agreement)

3. I will be ready for you at the appointed time. Please try to arrive on time, as I do not have a waiting room. If you arrive late for any reason the session will still finish at the appointed time.

4. I will take all reasonable precautions to keep our therapy space safe from interruption and intrusion, such as from telephone calls, deliveries and workmen, though there may be rare occasions when this is not feasible. I ask you to respect the therapy space, too, by not accepting mobile phone calls.

5. You have my phone number in case you need it. My telephone answering machine will usually be on if I am not available when you call and I will make every effort to return your call before the end of my working day. I am happy to be available to you, by prior agreement, for short telephone contact between sessions. If you need to speak to me for a prolonged length of time (more than 5 minutes) I will charge you *pro rata* for that time based on my session rate. I will also bill you on a pro rata basis for any reports that I may be required to write or to read in connection with your therapy.

6. Please avoid taking affect altering drugs or alcohol before a session.

7. I will take holidays during the year–usually in the summer period, at Christmas/New Year, and Easter/Passover, plus "half term" weeks where appropriate. I will let you know the dates well in advance.

8. It is my responsibility to monitor my health and fitness to work. This means that I may have to cancel a session at short notice due to illness or other unforeseen life events.

9. If you are unable to attend a session due to illness or unforeseen circumstances, please call and let me know, and we may be able to re-schedule. Please bear in mind, however, that such re-arrangement may not always be possible. My flexibility is limited by the fact that I see clients on a regular basis, at the same time and day each week, so alternative appointment times are not freely available, and Saturday mornings can be used only exceptionally. I will expect you to pay for any sessions you decide to miss altogether, as I cannot make any other use of "your time". If I am able to offer you an alternative appointment in the same week in which you need to cancel I will only charge you for the one session.

10. If you decide to cancel sessions due to *foreseen* circumstances, such as taking a holiday yourself or working away, please let me know at least 4 weeks in advance. I will then only charge you half the usual fee for sessions missed in this way. If you give me less notice than this, I will expect you to pay the full fee for any missed sessions. I will not attempt to re-schedule sessions in the above circumstances.

11. The therapeutic relationship is intended to be healing, supportive and sometimes challenging. We need to be aware that there may be times, as in any human relationship, when things feel difficult and it seems hard to persevere. These times, if worked through together, can be very fruitful and life-enhancing for you. We both need to have the intention of seeing things through in such circumstances.

12. If either of us thinks it is time to bring the therapy to an end, we will discuss this together and decide if and how to do that. Sometimes one session is enough to make sure the decision is a good one. Sometimes it is better to have a series of sessions to review the work and either decide to go on with therapy after all, or else to find a way of making a good ending for you. Ending the therapeutic relationship is a shared process and should never be a one-sided or impulsive act.

13. Everything that happens in our therapy session remains confidential between us, with the following exceptions:

    • I will discuss aspects of our work with other colleagues for supervisory purposes, but your identity will remain protected;

    • when required by law, which is very rare;

    • I may contact your GP or other medical professionals involved if I believe you are likely to cause serious injury to yourself or others.

14. Any addition agreements made between us:

Signed..(client)

Date...

Signed...(therapist)

Date...

Any comments or queries?

REFERENCES

Ainsworth, M.D.S., Blehar, M.C., Waters, E., & Wall, S. (1978). *Patterns of Attachment: A psychological study of the strange situation*. Hillsdale, NJ: Erlbaum.

American Psychiatric Association (1994). *Diagnostic and Statistical Manual of Mental Disorders* (4th ed.). Washington, DC: APA.

Balint, M (1968). *The Basic Fault*. London: Tavistock.

Barr, J. (1987). The therapeutic relationship model: Perspective on the core of the healing process. *Transactional Analysis Journal, 20*(4): 134–140.

Bauman, Z. (1993). *Postmodern ethics*. Oxford: Blackwells.

Bauman, Z. (1994). *Alone again: Ethics after certainty*. London: Demos.

Benjamin, L.S. (1996). *Interpersonal Diagnosis and Treatment of Personality Disorders, (2nd ed.)* New York: Guilford Press.

Berne, E. (1972). *What do you say after you say hello?: The psychology of human destiny*. New York: Grove Press.

Bion, W. (1959). Attacks on linking in *International Journal of Psycho-Analysis, 40*: 308–15.

Bion, W. (1962). *Learning from Experience*. London: Heinemann.

191

Bleger, J. (1967). Psychoanalysis of the Psycho-analytic Frame, *International Journal of Psycho-analysis, 48*: 511–519.

Bollas, C. (1987). *The Shadow of the Object.* London: Free Association Books.

Bond, T. (1993). *Standards and ethics for counselling in action.* London: Sage.

Bond, T. (2000). *Standards and ethics for counselling in action* (2nd ed.). London: Sage.

Bond, T. (2002). *The law of confidentiality–the solution or part of the problem.* In: Legal Issues in Counselling and Psychotherapy. Jenkins, P.(Ed.). London: Sage 2002.

Bond, T. (2004). *Ethical guidelines for researching counselling and psychotherapy.* Rugby: British Association for Counselling and Psychotherapy.

British Association for Counselling and Psychotherapy (2002). *Ethical Framework for good practice in counselling and psychotherapy.* Rugby, UK.

Bowlby, J. (1969). *Attachment and Loss, Vol. 1: Attachment.* London: Hogarth Press and the Institute of Psychoanalysis.

Bowlby, J. (1973). *Attachment and Loss, Vol. 2: Separation: Anxiety and Anger.* London: Hogarth Press and Institute of Psychoanalysis.

Buber, M. (1970). *I and Thou* (W. Kaufmann, Trans.). New York: Simon & Schuster. (Original work published 1957).

Casemore, R. (2001). "Managing boundaries–it's—the little things that count" in *Surviving Complaints Against Counsellors and Psychotherapists.* Casemore, R. (ed.) Ross-on-Wye: PCCS Books.

Cooper-White, P. (2001). The use of self in psychotherapy: A comparative study of pastoral counsellors and clinical social workers. In: *American Journal of Pastoral Counseling.* 4(4): 5–35.

Cornell, W.F. (2003). What am I getting myself into? *Transactional Analysis Journal, 33*: 4–14.

Cornell, W.F., & Bonds-White, F. (2005). Therapeutic relatedness in transactional analysis: The truth of love or the love of truth. In Cornell, W.F., & Hargaden, H., (Eds.), *From transactions to relations: The emergence of a relational tradition in transactional analysis* (pp. 135–151). Chadlingtron, Oxfordshire, England: Haddon Press. (Original work published 2001).

Cornell, W.F., & Hargaden, H. (2005). When the therapeutic relationship is at the heart of the work. In: Cornell, W.F., & Hargaden, H., (Eds.), *From transactions to relations: The emergence of a relational tradition in transactional analysis* (pp. 5–19). Chadlington, Oxfordshire, England: Haddon Press.

Diamond, M. (1993). *The Unconscious Life of Organisations*, London: Quorum.

Drego, P. (1983). The cultural parent. *Transactional Analysis Journal, 13:* 224–227.

Elkind, S.N. (1992). *Resolving Impasses in Therapeutic Relationships.* New York: Guilford Press.

Edmondson, Mary (2004). Reporting of termination of membership. In: *Counselling and Psychotherapy Journal, 15,*(6).

Fairbairn, W.R.D. (1952). *Psychoanalytic Studies of the Personality.* London: Routledge & Kegan Paul.

Firman, & Gila, (1997). *The Primal Wound: a transpersonal view of trauma, addiction and growth.* Albany, NY: State University of New York Press.

Fonagy, P., & Target, M. (1997). "Attachment and reflective function: Their role in self-organization". *Development and Psychopathology, 9,* 679–700.

Freud, S. (1900/2001). *The Interpretation of Dreams.* Standard Edition Vols. 4 & 5 London: Hogarth/Vintage Press.

Freud, S. (1913). On the beginning of treatment. In: *The Standard Edition of the Complete Works of Sigmund Freud, vol. 12,* translated and edited by Strachy, J. London: Hogarth Press (1958). pp. 123–144.

Freud, S. (1930/2001). *Civilisation and its Discontents* Standard Edition Vol. 21 London: Hogarth/Vintage Press.

Gabbard, G. (2000). Consultation from the consultant's perspective. In: *Psychoanalytic dialogues 10*(2): 209–218.

Gabbard, G. (2003). Miscarriages of psychoanalytic treatment with suicidal patients. Ontario: International Psychoanalytic Association Congress (*Key Note Address*).

Gabbard, Glen O., & Lester, Eva P. *Boundaries and Boundary Violations in Psychoanalysis*. N.Y.: Basic Books.

Gesitwhite, R. (2000). Inadequacy and indebetedness; no-fee psychotherapy in county training programs. In: *Journal of Psychotherapy Practice and Research* 9:142–148.

Goleman, D. (1996). *Emotional Intelligence*. London: Bloomsbury Publishing.

Gomez, L. (1997). *An Introduction to Object Relations*. London: Free Association Books.

Gordon Brown, I. (2002). *Journey in Depth*. Leicester: Archive Publishing.

Greenson, R.R. (1978). *Explorations in Psychoanalysis*. New York: International Universities Press.

Griffin, G. (2004). Professional conduct: what you need to know. In: *Counselling and Psychotherapy Journal*. 15(6): 46–47.

Guggenbuhl-Craig, A. (1968). *The Psychotherapist's Shadow*. In: Wheelwright, J. (ed). The Reality Principle, New York: Putnam's.

Guggenbuhl-Craig, A. (1971). *Power in the Helping Professions*, Zurich: Spring Publications.

Gutheil, T., & Gabbard, G. (1993). The concept of boundaries in clinical practice: theoretical and risk-management dimensions. In *American Journal of Psychiatry*. 150:188–96.

Guthiel, T., & Gabbard, G. (1998). Misuses and misunderstandings of boundary theory in clinical and regulatory settings. *American Journal of Psychiatry*. March, 155: 409–414.

Habermas, J. (1986). *Knowledge and human interest* (J.J. Shapiro, Trans.). Oxford: Polity Press.

Halpin, N. (2005). *The Supporter Type: is this you?* In: Therapy Today Sept. (2005). 16(07).

Hargaden, H., & Sills, C. (2002). *Transactional analysis: A relational perspective*. London: Brunner-Routledge.

Harris, E. A. (1995). "The importance of risk management in a managed care environment". In: *A Perilous Calling: The Hazards of Psychotherapy Practice*, ed. M.B. Sussman. New York: John Wiley and Sons.

Heath. S. (1991). *Dealing with the Therapist's Vulnerability to Depression*. London: Jason Aaronson.

Hebb. D. (1949). *The Organization of Experience: A Neuropsychological Theory*. New York: Wiley.

Herman, J. (1992). *Trauma and Recovery*. New York: Basic Books.

Herron, W.G., & Rouslin Welt, S. (1992). *Money Matters: The Fee in Psychotherapy and Psychoanalysis*. New York: Guilford Press.

House, R., & Totton, N. (Eds.) (1997). *Implausible Professions: Arguments for Pluralism and Autonomy in Psychotherapy and Counselling*. Ross-on-Wye: PCCS Books.

Huffington, C., Armstrong, D., Halton, W., Hoyle, L., & Pooley, J. (2004). *Working below the Surface*. London: Karnac.

Hycner, R. & Jacobs, L. (1995). *The Healing Relationship in Gestalt Therapy*. Highland, NY: The Gestalt Journal Press.

Janis, I. (1982). *Groupthink*. Boston: Houghton Mifflin.

Johnson, S.M. (1994). *Character Styles*. New York: Norton.

Johnstone, G. (2003). *A Restorative Justice Reader*. Oregon: Willan Publishing.

Jonsen, A.R. (1999). *A short history of medical ethics*. New York: Oxford University Press.

Jung C.G. (1938). *Psychology and Religion*. Collected Works (1953). London: Routledge and Kegan Paul.

Jutte R. (1999). Thus it passes from the patient's purse into that of the doctor without causing displeasure—Samuel Hahnemann and medical fees. *Med. Ges. Gesch.* 18: 149–67.

Kearns, A. (2005). *The Seven Deadly Sins?–Issues in Clinical Practice and Supervision for Humanistic and Integrative Practitioners*. London: Karnac.

Kearns, A., & Daintry, P. (2000). Shame in the supervisory relationship: living with the enemy. *British Gestalt Journal*, 9(1):28–38.

Kernberg, O. (1998). *Ideology, Conflict, and Leadership in Groups and Organisations*. London: Yale University Press.

Klebanow, S., & Lowenkopf, E. L. (1991). *Money and Mind*. New York: Plenum Press.

Klein, M. (1945). *Love, Guilt and Reparation* London: Hogarth/Virago Press.

Kohut, H. (1977). *The Restoration of the Self*. New York: International Universities Press.

Kohut, H. (1982). Introspection, empathy and the semi-circle of mental health. *International Journal of Psychoanalysis, 63*: 395–407.

Kohut, H. (1984). *How does analysis cure?* Chicago: University of Chicago Press.

Lambert, M.J. (1992). Implications of outcome research for psychotherapy integration. Norcross, J.C., & Goldfried, M.R. *Handbook of Psychotherapy Integration*, pp. 94–129.

Lapworth, P. (2003). *Introjective transference in working with gay, lesbian and bi-sexual clients, who are addressing their sexual identity.* Presentation at the conference of the Institute of Transactional Analysis, Swansea, Wales.

Lee, R.G., (Eds.) (2004). *The Values of Connection: a relational approach to ethics.* Cambridge, MA: Gestalt Press.

Lewin, K. (1952). *Field Theory in Social Science.* London: Tavistock.

Kroll, J. (1993). PTSD/Borderlines in Therapy: Finding the Balance. New York: Norton.

Krueger, D., (Eds.) (1986). *The Last Taboo; Money as Symbol and Reality in Psychotherapy and Psychoanalysis.* New York: Brunner/Mazel.

Main, M., & Solomon, J. (1986). Discovery of an insecure-disorganized/disoriented pattern. In: Brazelton, T.B., & Yogman, M., (Eds.). *Affective Development in Infancy.* Norwood, NJ: Ablex Publishing.

Mann, D. (1997). *Psychotherapy: An Erotic Relationship.* London: Brunner-Routledge.

Maslow, A. (1968). *Toward a Psychology of Being.* New York: Van Nostrand.

Masterson, J.F. (1986). *The Search for the Real Self: Unmasking the Personality Disorders of Our Age.* New York: The Free Press.

McGrath, G. (1994). Ethics, boundaries and contracts: Applying moral principles. *Transactional Analysis Journal, 24*, 6–14.

Menzies Lyth, I. (1993). *The Dynamics of the Social: Selected Essays.* London: Free Association Books.

Messler-Davies, J. (2003). *Falling in Love with Love.* New York: Psychoanalytic Dialogues *13*(1): 1–27.

Miller, A. (1981). *The Drama of Being a Child.* London: Virago.

Milner, M. (1952). Aspects of Symbolism and Comprehension of the Not-Self, *International Journal of Psycho-analysis, 33*: 181–85.

Murray, R.M., Pugh, J.L. & Clance. P.R. (2004). The ethics of touch and imagery in psychotherapy: a gestalt resolution. In: *The Values of Connection*, R.G. Lee (Ed.). Cambridge MA: The Gestalt Press.

Myers, D. (2005). *Therapist Self-disclosure of Countertransference: necessity or indulgence?* American Psychological Society Division 32 website.

Nathanson, D. (1992). *Shame and Pride: Affect, Sex and the Birth of the Self.* New York: Norton.

Nhat Hanh, T. (1987). *The Miracle of Mindfulness.* Boston: Beacon Press.

Oakley, A. (2005). *The Ann Oakley reader: Gender, women and social science.* Bristol: Policy Press.

O'Neill, O. (2002). *Autonomy and Trust in Bioethics.* Cambridge: Cambridge University Press.

O'Shea, L. (2000). Sexuality: old struggles and new challenges. *Gestalt Review.* 4(1): 8–25.

Palmer Barnes, F. (1998). *Complaints and Grievances in Psychotherapy. A Handbook of Ethical Practice.* London: Sage.

Pappworth, M.H. (1967). *Human guinea pigs: Experimentation on man.* Boston: Beacon Press.

Peperzak, A.T., Critchley, S., & Bernasconi, R. (Eds.). (1996). *Emmanuel Levinas: Basic philosophical readings.* Bloomington, IN: Indiana University Press.

Perls, F., Hefferline, R., & Goodman, P. (1951). *Gestalt Therapy: Excitement and Growth in the Human Personality.* (1984 ed.). London: Souvenir Press.

Perraton Mountford, C. (2005). *One size does not fit all.* CPJ June.

Peterson, M.R. (1992). *At Personal Risk: Boundary violations in Professional-Client Relationships.* New York: W.W. Norton.

Philippson, P. (2002). Contemporary Challenges in the Application of Perls' Five-Layer Theory. In: *Gestalt!* ISSN 1091-1766 6(2).

Popper, K. (1959). *The logic of scientific discovery.* New York: Basic Books.

Postle, D. (1998). The alchemist's nightmare: gold into lead—the annexation of psychotherapy in the UK. *International Journal of Psychotherapy.* 3: 53–83.

Postle, D. (2000). Statutory regulation: Shrink-wrapping psychotherapy. *British Journal of Psychotherapy, 16*(3): 335–46.

Putnam, F.W. (1997). *Dissociation in Children and Adolescents: A developmental perspective.* New York: Guilford Press.

Robertson, C. (1993). *Dysfunction In Training Organisation.* In: Self and Society. *21*(4).

Rogers, C. (1942). *Counselling and Psychotherapy.* New York: Houghton Mifflin.

Rogers, C. (1951). *Client Centred Therapy.* London: Constable.

Rothschild, B. (2000). T*he Body Remembers: The Psychophysiology of Trauma and Trauma Treatment.* New York: Norton.

Rowan, J. (2001). *Ordinary Ecstasy: The Dialectics of Humanistic Psychology* (3rd ed.) London: Brunner/Routledge.

Rutter, P. (1991). *Sex in the Forbidden Zone.* New York: Fawcett.

Schiff, J.L., & Day, B. (1970). *All My Children.* New York: Pyramid.

Schore, A.N. (1994). *Affect Regulation and the Origin of the Self: The Neurobiology of Emotional Development.* Mahwah, NJ: Erlbaum.

Schore, A.N. (2001). The effects of early relational trauma on right brain development, affect regulation and infant mental health. In: *Infant Mental Health Journal, 22*(1–2): 7–66.

Sedgwick, D. (1994). *The Wounded Healer.* London: Routledge.

Seinfeld, J. (1990). *The Empty Core: An Object Relations Approach to Psychotherapy with the Schizoid Personality.* New Jersey: Aronson.

Shadbolt, C. (2004). Homophobia and gay affirmative transactional analysis. *Transactional Analysis Journal, 34*:207–210.

Shaw, R. (2003). *The Embodied Therapist: The Therapist's Body Story.* Hove and New York: Brunner-Routledge.

Siegel, D. (1999). *The Developing Mind: Toward a Neurobiology of Interpersonal Experience.* New York: Guilford Press.

Sivyer, J. (2000). Complaints: the search for restorative justice, *Self & Society, 28*(1): 13–21.

Stern, D.B. (1998). Not misusing empathy. *Contemporary Psychoanalysis, 24*: 598–611.

Stern, D. (2004). *The Present Moment in Psychotherapy & Everyday Life.* London: W. W. Norton & Co Ltd.

Stigler J.G. (1971). The Theory of Economic Regulation, *Bell Journal of Economics and Management Science*, 2: 3–21.

Stolorow, R. & Atwood, G. (1979). *Faces in a Cloud: Subjectivity in Personality Theory*. Northvale, NJ: Jason Aronson.

Stokoe, P., & Fisher, J. (1997). An invitation to a dialogue about a model for a complaints procedure, *Society of Psychoanalytic Marital Psychotherapists Bulletin*, 4: 51–55.

Storr, A. (1999). *The Art of Psychotherapy*. London: Routledge.

Thompson, A. (1990). *Guide to ethical practice in psychotherapy*. New York: Wiley.

Tomkins, S.S. (1962). *Affect Imagery Consciousness, Vol. I*. New York: Springer.

Totton, N. (1999). The baby and the bathwater: professionalisation in psychotherapy and counselling. *British Journal of Guidance and Counselling*, 27(3): 313–24.

Totton. N. (2001). Scapegoats and sacred cows: towards good enough conflict resolution. *Surviving Complaints Against counsellors and Psychotherapists*. Casemore, R. (Ed.). Ross-on-Wye: PCCS Books.

Trachtman (1999). The money taboo: Its effects in everyday life and in the practice of psychotherapy. *Clinical Social Work Journal*, 27(3):275-288.

Trumble, W.R., & Stevenson, A. (Eds.). (2002). *The Shorter Oxford English Dictionary on Historical Principles*. Oxford: Oxford University Press.

Tudor, K., & Worrall, M. (2006). *Person-Centred Therapy: A Clinical Philosophy*. London: Routledge.

Van der Kolk, B. (1989). The Compulsion to Repeat The Trauma: Re-enactment, revictimiszation and masochism. *Psychiatric Clinics of North America*, 12(2): 389–411.

Walton, M. (2005). It ain't what you do it's the way that you do it..?–or is it? Some ponderings on how Leadership will go astray. Paper for 6th Conference on HRD Research and Practice Across Europe.

Winnicott, D. (1949). Hate in the countertransference. *International Journal of Psychoanalysis* 30: 67–74.

Winnicott, D. (1965). *Maturational Processes & the Facilitative Environment*. London: Karnac Books.

Winnicott, D. (1967). Mirror role of mother and family in child development. In: *The Predicament of the Family*, Peter Lomas (Ed.). London:
Hogarth Press.

Yalom, I. (1980). *Existential Psychotherapy*. New York: Basic Books.

Zinker, J. (1977). *Creative Process in Gestalt Therapy*. New York: Random
House.

INDEX

This index is in word-by-word order. Page numbers in *italics* refer to case studies and examples; page numbers followed by 'n' indicate a note.